*Proceedings of the Carondelet
Conference on*

THE FUTURE OF RELIGIOUS LIFE

*M. Charlotte Marshall, O.S.P.
Angela Berríos, O.S.B.
Mary L. O'Hara, C.S.J.
Mary Ewens, O.P.
Ritamary Bradley, S.F.C.C.
Joseph Schmidt, F.S.C.
M. Clare Adams, O.S.C.
Vilma Seelaus, O.C.D.*

*Edited by Dolores Steinberg, O.S.C.
  with the assistance of
  Mary L. O'Hara, C.S.J
  and Helen Coughlan, C.S.J.*

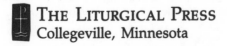

THE LITURGICAL PRESS
Collegeville, Minnesota

Cover design by Mary Furth.

1   2   3   4   5   6   7   8   9   10

Library of Congress Cataloging-in-Publication Data

Carondelet Conference on the Future of Religious Life (1988 : College of St. Catherine)
    Proceedings of the Carondelet Conference on the Future of Religious Life / essays by Mary Charlotte Marshall . . . [et al.] ; edited by Dolores Steinberg with the assistance of Mary L. O'Hara and Helen Coughlan.
      p. cm.
    Includes bibliographical references.
    ISBN 0-8146-1908-8
    1. Monastic and religious life—Congresses. 2. Monasticism and religious orders—Congresses. I. Marshall, Mary Charlotte, 1927–
II. Steinberg, Dolores. III. O'Hara, Mary Louise R. IV. Coughlan, Helen. V. Title. VI. Title: Future of religious life.
BX2435.C275 1988   89-78200
255-dc20   CIP

Contents

To the valiant men and women with whom we have walked, to those in whose footsteps we trod, and to those who will follow us in faith and hope; and to Our Lady of Guadalupe, pregnant virgin, patroness of the Americas, and sign of hope for the oppressed everywhere.

Preface

On three halcyon days of Pentecost weekend, 1988, eight religious met at Carondelet Center in St. Paul, Minnesota, to consider the future of religious life.

The grassroots effort to discern in the present the seeds of future growth for religious communities brought seven sisters and one Christian Brother to the former novitiate building of the Sisters of St. Joseph. There in a setting reminiscent of the past they considered imperatives for the future.

Both past and future came into sharp focus in the last few minutes of the formal sessions. Is it wise to go back over the events of the past several years in searching for new directions? This is what the Jews do in celebrating their Passover: "Our ancestors were slaves in Egypt." And Christian liturgy picks up the theme in telling the story not of the resurrection alone but also of the suffering and death of Jesus.

Again, what is the "present"? Is the present a *point*, a nonextended, evanescent moment? Or is it a *period of time*, an extent, this present year or day or any other spread-out length of time? In the first case the changing present is constantly being replaced by what until that moment was a "future." In the second case the future, seen as a stretch of time, say the last decade of this century, may seem not to impinge directly upon the present in which we find ourselves.

Should religious today use words like "oppressive" or "life-denying" in speaking of past aberrations? Or is it more

5

advisable, at least rhetorically, to emphasize the positive and, beginning from where we now are, from the present year for example, and neglecting the undoubted fact that half of it is already past and the other half future, to try to discern in it the seeds of growth and life and to nurture these and let what seems not to promise life wither?

M. Clare Adams, O.S.C., pointed out that we need to tell our stories to be faithful to our tradition. One of the great lacks at present in Christian liturgy, she said, is a place for lamentation. Instead of an official, *public* lamentation (which is one of the two great categories of psalms, the other being that of celebration; and each of these, entered into deeply enough, turns into the other), we bring our private laments into the general intercessions.

Constraints of time prevented a resolution of this conflict of ideas; but much of value had already taken place in the course of the three days. These *Proceedings* are an attempt to bring to a wider audience a feel for what happened during the conference and some of the principal things the participants learned.

Throughout the conference there was completely open sharing; we learned with surprise about common interests, acquaintances, and background. Thus, it turned out that four of the participants were alumnae of The College of Saint Catherine. Two proved to be native Philadelphians with common acquaintances. Two had worked on a national and international level in early phases of the movement to renew religious communities. In few of these cases, however, had participants been acquainted previous to this meeting.

Participants came from many religious traditions, reaching from the Benedictine, rooted in ancient times, to the twentieth-century Sisters for Christian Community. There were besides a Carmelite, a Christian Brother, a Dominican, an Oblate of Divine Providence, a Poor Clare, and a Sister of St.

Joseph. All spoke in slightly different tongues (and Vespers on Pentecost Eve was celebrated in Spanish as well as English), and everyone made a sustained effort to speak candidly and listen carefully to what was being said by others.

The format of the conference followed guidelines issued with the invitation: that everyone should have read all the papers before the conference and that each participant should be asked to present his or her thoughts on the subject in ten or fifteen minutes, after which general discussion would ensue. A record of the actual discussion was kept on audio and videotape for the assistance of the editor of the proceedings.

Setting up the conference with a minimum of outside assistance was a calculated risk, taken in an effort to model a possible future mode of religious life. Thus the meals, instead of being catered, were prepared by participants, under the supervision of Sister Clare; videotaping was accomplished by Mary L. O'Hara, C.S.J., after receiving initial help in setting up equipment from Kathleen Holmberg, C.S.J., and Maureen Lamey, C.S.J. Ritamary Bradley, S.F.C.C., supervised the audiorecording with help from other participants, and Vilma Seelaus, O.C.D., and Joseph Schmidt, F.S.C., along with other participants, gave help in the kitchen at crucial moments. Eileen Dutton, C.S.J., baked a memorable fresh rhubarb pie, Karen Wadsworth, C.S.J., assisted with reception of guests, Catherine Kessler, C.S.J., helped run errands upon request, and the staff of the Carondelet Center, including Gertrude Marie Keltgen, C.S.J., Grace Saumer, C.S.J., and Ernesta Mahlmann, C.S.J., were uniformly helpful. Joan McGinty, C.S.J, provided photocopy assistance in preparing the papers for publication. A poster made by Jo Casey, O.S.C., proclaimed that "Hope has two lovely daughters, anger and courage; anger so that what must not be, may not be; courage, so that what should be, can be" (St. Augustine).

The point of all this activity was to model to some extent

the kind of religious life that may and perhaps should emerge in the years to come. Thus when Doris Rauenhorst, O.P., vicar for religious of the Archdiocese of St. Paul and Minneapolis, sat with participants at breakfast the second day of the conference and said "I don't want to make you late for your meeting," the answer was, "This IS the meeting."

Karen Kennelly, C.S.J., provincial superior of the Sisters of St. Joseph of Carondelet, who had encouraged the project from the beginning, welcomed delegates the first evening with a survey of the situation as it appeared to her.

She emphasized that she had come in the past twenty years to recognize the limitations of the scholarly approach to questions; however, meetings like this one are important at present when great changes in society and Church seem to be bringing about truly radical changes in religious life. Think of the Reformation: how so many religious houses were emptied with so little record being left.

Despite these great changes (great reductions in numbers of Benedictines in the sixteenth to eighteenth centuries, for example), still there remains a great toughness in religious life. Hence, there is great value of such a meeting as this one, a very exciting venture. She closed with the remark that a meeting in St. Louis led by Gerald A. Arbuckle, S.M., on refounding religious life had just ended, and she asked the Holy Spirit to bless this meeting.

This was followed by participants' presentations in the order that seemed appropriate in light of themes that were emerging. The first evening Charlotte Marshall, O.S.P., dealt with racism in religious communities. The following morning Angela Berríos, O.S.B., speaking from the viewpoint of one who experiences colonialism every day, called attention to the fact that, paradoxically, instead of trying to become or remain part of the mainstream of society, we Christians must all become marginalized and so join the poor in their marginalization. Sisters Clare and Vilma spoke of attempts to update contemplative religious life, and Sister Ritamary spoke of the early history of bureaucratic opposition to American sisters' taking control of their own destiny. Mary Ewens, O.P., reflected upon the findings of the Quinn Commission; Brother Joseph identified life-giving elements in the newer religious experience, such as "quality time" spent with the community.

The Pentecost liturgy at the Monastery of Saint Clare in Minneapolis renewed some old ties and forged new ones with the community and laypersons present.

In the final paper, Sister Mary dealt with philosophical aspects of issues regarding the future, including Plotinus' statement that for a noneternal being, a future is necessary for one's very being. Discussion of the paper and concluding remarks ended shortly after noon that day.

Common themes emerged in several papers: for example, themes of charism, of contemplation, of hope, of problems of marginality, of image, and of women. Another frequently addressed question was that of how religious relate to others: the poor, lay members of the Church, non-Christians, etc.

One point which occasioned some sharp discussion was that of the advisability of establishing a center to study questions regarding the future of religious life on a continuing basis. The statement that already existing organizations, such as the Leadership Conference of Women Religious (LCWR) and the Center for Applied Research in the Apostolate (CARA), are taking care of this was met by the counterclaim that these organizations do not necessarily impact upon all religious communities, that it has taken the LCWR a long time to get around to considering, for example, racism in religious communities, and that the sorts of questions religious most need to focus upon are sapiential, not easily formulated for hard data scientific research. These are emerging, barely noticeable trends that may carry the germ of the survival of classic religious life into the future. Lack of time prevented adequate discussion, much less resolution, of this question, which is nevertheless recognized to be crucial.

I wish to thank Dolores Steinberg, O.S.C., who generously gave of the time she could spare from duties as abbess of the Monastery of Saint Clare in Minneapolis to edit these papers, and Helen Coughlan, C.S.J., and Mary Anthony Wagner, O.S.B., who assisted her.

Finally, gratitude is due to the Sisters of St. Joseph of Carondelet, St. Paul Province, who demonstrated their faith in the project and their hope for the future of religious life by sponsoring this meeting, and to Mrs. Rosemary Hampston who generously contributed to its funding.

Mary L. O'Hara, C.S.J.

St. Paul, Minnesota, Trinity Sunday, May 21, 1989

Part I
Cries of Oppression

In order to create the desired tomorrow, religious communities of predominantly white women must change racist patterns and begin new collaborative efforts with women of Afro-American heritage. This is the message of M. Charlotte Marshall, O.S.P., Baltimore, Maryland, currently superior general of the Oblate Sisters of Providence. In her paper Sister Charlotte recounts the racist conditions under which religious life was opened to Black women in the United States, conditions which she finds still exist, though in different forms. She concludes on a note of hope that, by accepting one another's rich cultural gifts and developing new modes of shared ministry, a renewed enthusiasm for religious life will be born.

1

"So Stood Those Who Have Come Down Through the Ages" . . . And Those Who Continue

M. Charlotte Marshall, O.S.P.

Afro-American women who have a commitment to vowed life in the Catholic Church in this century need the same courage and resolution to carry out that commitment today as their founders and foremothers needed to establish communites for Black women in the last century. I take the title for my reflections on this subject from a pastoral letter on the family in the Black community written by Auxiliary Bishop James P. Lyke of Cleveland: "So Stood Those Who Have Come Down Through the Ages."[1] But I add, ". . . And Those Who Continue," for my concern is with what has transpired in the Catholic Church since those early years in the United States for women of Afro-American heritage.

The Black bishops of the United States, in their pastoral letter on evangelization, "What We Have Seen and Heard," note that there were Black women religious in the United States before there were any Black Catholic priests.[2] The founder of my own community, Elizabeth Lange, was a free Black living in Baltimore in the 1820s. She became aware of the deplorable conditions in which free Blacks were living. Like herself, many of them were French-speaking Caribbean immigrants who found it nearly impossible to obtain work in a slave society,

13

and what work was to be found was underpaid. Since many of them were Catholic, she wanted to help them by giving their children rudimentary education along with religious instruction.

She was not eligible, of course, to enter the Daughters of Charity, the only apostolic community for women then established in the United States. Her advisor recommended that she, with three other Black women, establish a community. To do so she had to overcome the objection of the bishop of Baltimore, who agreed with many of his white flock that Black women were not worthy to wear the religious habit.

The community of the Oblate Sisters of Providence was nevertheless successfully established and received official recognition by the Church in 1831, two years after it was founded. Establishment as a religious congregation did not mean the end of opposition, however, whether open or subtle. Until the 1950s the community never received a request for sisters to work except at places which other communities had abandoned. Moreover, they were usually told when invited that they could not expect to receive the same stipend offered to white religious.

After noting the contribution of Elizabeth Lange and her leadership within the Black Catholic community "in the hostile environment of Baltimore," the Black bishops draw attention also to other courageous Black women:

> Evangelization among the Blacks of New Orleans was also the task assumed by Henriette Delille, who in the face of crushing opposition founded the Sisters of the Holy Family in 1842. These two Black congregations of religious women were joined by a third in our own century when Mother Theodore Williams helped establish the Franciscan Handmaids of the Most Pure Heart of Mary in 1916 in Savannah, Georgia.[3]

All these women and those who have followed them up to the present day give testimony to the world of what can happen when women dedicate themselves to lives totally committed to the prophetic words of Scripture. It would be most gratifying if I could affirm that life is better today for Afro-American women religious and for all other minorities in the United States. You and I know well, however, that this is not the truth.

The noted American Catholic historian Fr. John Tracy Ellis states emphatically that "one of the saddest chapters in the Catholic story in the United States is to be found in the Church's relationship to the Black community."[4] He goes on to quote John LaFarge, S.J., who observed that "the tragedy is not so much in the mistakes that were made but that positive, bold, and constructive steps were not taken at a much earlier date."[5] Yet the work of Father LaFarge to keep Blacks in the Catholic Church, first in southern Maryland and later in New York, met with opposition from the clergy and even from members of his own community.

Recent popes have given support and hope to the aspirations of Black Catholics. In his address at Kampala in Uganda in 1969, Pope Paul VI urged his listeners: ". . . enrich the Church with your unique gift of Blackness." During his visit to the United States in September 1987, Pope John Paul II clearly expressed his identification with the aims of Black Americans: "Know that the pope stands united with the black community as it rises to embrace its full dignity and lofty destiny."[6] While in New Orleans he expressed "deep love and esteem" and urged Black Catholics to "keep alive and active" their rich cultural gifts.[7] He continued: "Your black cultural heritage enriches the Church and makes her witness of universality more complete. In a real way the church needs you, just as you need the church, for you are part of the church and the church is part of you."[8]

When Pope John Paul addressed these words to the assembled Black Catholics in New Orleans, the group's response was overwhelming. Although the security forces had given instructions not to stand because of the crowded conditions, all rose spontaneously to applaud. It was the very first time any church leader had recognized Blacks as an integral and necessary part of the Church.

Now the questions remain. Will there be a change in attitudes of white Catholics? Will these "rich cultural gifts" now be accepted? Will positive, bold, and constructive steps be taken to change the status quo?

All that Pope John Paul II has said to the universal Church needs to be said to religious communities. *We must change in order to create the desired tomorrow.* Young Black women are still desirous of dedicating themselves in service to the Church through vowed commitment. True, the proportion of Black women who show interest in religious life is not as great as that of white women, but there are some. Among the few who are accepted into programs of formation in religious life, even fewer remain. Of these, too many find they are unable to continue because, in the religious community itself, they have encountered a total lack of awareness of the history or culture of the Black woman's life and a consequent insensitivity to her needs. Some Black women remain in religious life, but at the price of "changing" their culture or by ignoring the problem or by trying to deal with it by constructing other names for it. This method of coping causes a serious diminution in creativity and in the realization of one's optimum potential and reduces the ability to live a life of prayer and service. If anyone doubts the reality of this description of the condition of Black women integrated into white religious communities, it might be helpful to remember that the Conference of Black Religious was founded by Black women in predominantly white communities to deal with their problems of cultural alienation.

There is no better time than now for us to intensify our efforts and attune our thoughts to the urgency of the need to eliminate racism from our families, Church congregations, student populations, and religious communities. For the last are by no means exempt from this evil. It is not uncommon, even in these days, for the superiors of Black communities to receive a letter from another community naming a "fine Black girl" who wishes to become a religious. When I receive such a letter, my first question is "Have you invited her to join your community?" Is it not the responsibility of those of us already committed to gospel values to blaze the path for those hoping to share the role of leadership in the Catholic community and to assist them in using their gifts of intellect and spirit for the cause of Christ? Our response to that challenge will test and determine our authenticity.

Socrates was the first of many spiritual leaders to say, "An unexamined life is not worth living." We must, as women hastening toward the third millennium, make an honest appraisal of our position on racism in order to blend vision, courage, and reason with our life of serious personal commitment. An unknown writer has warned us:

> The future of the past is in the present.
> The future of the present is in the future.
> The future of the future is in the past.
> So be very careful about your past.

Our racist past is a formidable barometer of what the future will be if we do not take steps to change it. We must begin now to make sure that the future will not become a time of retrogression.

We are now at a crossroads and must make grave decisions about our course of direction. According to Patricia McCann, R.S.M., the future of religious life "is likely to be very different in form and structure from both past and present."[9] With all the creative potential latent in our communities, rich in cultural diversity, we have a tremendous resource for sharing ministries that will include all our members. Working together side by side can bring about a new creation. Such collaboration will require of us new strategies so that all will feel comfortable with the plan of sharing such wisdom.

Many new spiritual, educational, and social programs are already operative throughout the country to the enrichment of religious life. Intercommunity sharing of new works will be a rich experience too, not only for ourselves but also for those we serve, especially the poor. One such operation in which my own community is involved is the New Community in Newark, New Jersey. This nonprofit corporation serves people whose ages range from the very young to the senior citizen. Special service is given to persons who are differently abled, physically or mentally, to those who have been subjected to violence and abuse, to persons terminally ill, and to persons with low income. For the latter, meals are shared economically in a renovated church setting. Enabling all participants to engage in wholistic living, no matter what their financial status, is a goal of the New Community corporation.

Let us hope that, using our concerted wisdom and efforts enhanced by a new enthusiasm, American religious can establish a Center for the Future of Religious Life. Such a center could serve as a resource of information in the area, for example, of new ministries needed not only by neglected members of society but also by religious communities in need of revitalization. The corporate reflection now being engaged in and subsequent planning will produce a viable mode for shared ministry.

Marjorie Wisor, O.S.F., in her article "How to Revitalize Religious Life," refers to an important point made by Loughlan Sofield, S.T., when he addressed their community chapter: "Each of us is uniquely gifted to help build the new creation, but our gifts are to be used in a collaborative ministry."[10] Sister Marjorie adds: "No longer are we as religious at the center of a carefully organized Church. Rather, we find ourselves, with the rest of the people of God, at the exciting, though anxiety-provoking, point of evolving towards the completely transformed body of Christ.''[11]

Eradicating the tenets of racism in our Church and in our communities and coming to that ''convergence of humanity towards the omega-point of the universe in Jesus, the God-Man''[12] will we, in Sister Marjorie's words, ''. . . believe in the extraordinary future to which we as religious are being called, will we be able to restrain ourselves from rushing out into the highways and byways of our world to share this call with enthusiasm and renewed belief in religious life''?[13]

All will be made NEW in Christ!

Notes

1. James P. Lyke, ''So Stood Those Who Have Come Down Through the Ages,'' A Pastoral Reflection on the Family in the Black Community, November 1986. See *Origins* 16, no. 28 (December 25, 1986) 511–16.

2. Black Bishops of the United States, *What We Have Seen and Heard: A Pastoral Letter on Evangelization* (Cincinnati: St. Anthony Messenger Press, September 9, 1984) 13.

3. *Ibid.* 13–14.

4. John Tracy Ellis, ''Episcopal Vision in 1884 and Thereafter,'' *U.S. Catholic Historian* 4, nos. 3 and 4 (1985) 204.

5. *Ibid.* 204.

6. Pope John Paul II, *Address to Black Catholics*, New Orleans, September 12, 1987. See *Origins* 17, no. 15 (September 24, 1987) 252.

7. *Ibid.* 251.

8. *Ibid.* 252.

9. Patricia McCann, ''The Future of Religious Life,'' *Sisters Today* 59, no. 2 (October 1987) 80.

10. Marjorie Wisor, ''How to Revitalize Religious Life,'' *Sisters Today* 59, no. 2 (October 1987) 98.

11. *Ibid.* 101–02.

12. *Ibid.* 101.

13. *Ibid.* 102.

*A*lthough Spanish is her native language, Angela Berríos, O.S.B, now regional superior of the Benedictine Sisters in Puerto Rico, writes here in English, speaking from her experience as director of formation for her sisters of the Priory of Santa Escolástica, Humacao, Puerto Rico, a dependent priory of the Sisters of St. Benedict in St. Joseph, Minnesota.

Hers is an important voice, calling for a return to the contemplative experience from which religious institutes were born and by which they will continue. "We need to rediscover the religious life as a spiritual movement," Sister Angela writes. Other significant points she makes are that if religious institutes are to meet the challenge of moving into the future, they will need to become real families, be more continually available to those who suffer injustice, and be consciously linked with the dynamism of the Church. She draws attention to the different theologies operative in shaping religious life: "The theology of the First World emphasizes the transcendent character of religious life in a secular world, while the theology of the Third World, particularly in Latin America, emphasizes the prophetic dimension of religious life in an unjust world." She also notes the contribution to the future of religious life being made by religious in Africa, Asia, and Latin America.

2

Religious Life *Ahora y Manana,* Today and Tomorrow

Angela Berríos, O.S.B.

We are in a great moment of time. We stand in the present but look ahead to the ways the Spirit will continue the history of religious life. To foresee the future is not easy, nor is it a simple matter to grasp what has happened to religious life since Vatican Council II. But we know we are on our way, walking with the Church which the Lord guides and enlightens. In trust, we have put ourselves into the hands of God.

The door opened to religious women and men by Vatican II has been a new point of departure, a moment that can be decisive because it carries within itself the seeds of the future. And it is of great value to focus attention on the future. The first postconciliar moments of the mid-1960s and 1970s were, without doubt, days of seeing more clearly toward the future. There is no doubt, however, that the last decade has been marked by confusion, some disillusion, stagnation, a nostalgic tendency toward the past, and excessive polarization. The rhythm of the religious life has been reduced, in many instances, merely to a process of renovation. Religious life needs to recover its heart, that contemplative center from which flows an eschatological vision of the future. Such vision deepens the

21

faith that nourishes enthusiasm and sustains the hope of the grain of wheat that falls into the ground and dies, but in dying, brings forth much fruit (see John 12:24).

To consider the future of religious life is not only good and necessary; it is indispensable. What we are hoping for, in some way, is an expression of what religious life really is. Such hope obligates us to formulate what we believe about religious life; recuperate inspired energies; verify, make precise, and confirm what has come from the past and make it significant and relevant to religious life today. As we focus on the future of religious life, some concerns may arise: Where will these ways of renovation take us in the coming years? What forms will they take in their concrete realization? Will those forms express the vital characteristics of Christian being that are presupposed by the nature of religious life itself?

Perhaps the greatest difficulty comes from the fear or anxiety about how we are going to accomplish all this. The final outcome will be given to us by God, and with it our creativity, our courage, and the gospel simplicity of the poor. Such an anticipated and assured outcome will open the world and the faithful to the eternal Word, who has pitched his tent in our midst. The founders of our various religious orders and congregations likewise have given witness in our midst, drawing their orientation from the life of the Church. This can give us direction as we run our own stretch now.

Vatican Council II has been a prophetic sign of God's intervention in our history, an act of love for the human race. It has also left its mark on religious life, a mark displaying all the characteristics of spiritual work: initial confusion, novelty, dynamism, missionary openness, liberty, pluralism, universality, communion, joy. But the council also wanted to offer to religious life a solemn moment of discernment. This invitation to discernment might be expressed through a critical question: "Religious life, what can you say about yourself?"

Before taking up the question of the future of religious life, I would like to take some time to answer the question posed by Vatican II, to say something about the nature of religious life and the context in which it is lived. There are four key points I would make:

1. Vatican Council II marks not a conclusion but a beginning

Vatican II is not the last step of yesterday but the first step of tomorrow. It is an ecclesial spring that offers to religious life new energy and, with it, the dream and the hope of much fruit.

2. Religious life is in serious crisis

In trying to look for new ways and paths, religious life has come into serious crisis, a crisis that precedes revitalization, or else weakening or disappearance. For each institute this crisis can be a vital moment, depending on whether it is willing and able to pay the price for the new life encouraged by the council. Some institutes have met these crises with a kind of "bloodless revolution"—by deciding to live and express the evangelical values in structures that are significant and clear for the world today.

3. Religious life is between crisis and hope

Where has religious life moved in the postconciliar period? I believe that since the council religious life has been in a situation between crisis and hope. All of us have taken part in this purification, although we have not necessarily made decisions at the same time or decided to do things in the same manner.

4. We must learn to link the life of the group to what makes it fruitful

The general impression at the present moment is that religious life is alive but is lacking sufficient vitality. Many of us may need to take a final step: to learn to link the life of the group to what makes it fruitful. The form of religious life should be suited to what is central to it: communicating the gift it has received to other followers of Christ. This will be accomplished when religious life is lived not as something marginal to the Church but when its form of being human and Christian is grounded in its growth in Jesus Christ.

* * *

Religious women and men of the third millennium will not be much different from the religious we aspire to be in 1990. Toward what might we move? There are several characteristics that I hope will be prominent in the religious life of the future:

1. That religious life be lived as a spiritual movement and from a spiritual movement

Religious life is a spiritual gift in the Church for the world. Its contemplative source, inspiration, and charism are embodied in a form of life that engenders attitudes, practices, and exercises. A religious vocation is above all an interior adventure of giving oneself to God and finding personal fullness in a concrete way. Women and men who join us are not looking for efficient and well-administered institutions. They are looking for persons and communities who in their words, conduct, and work radiate a spirituality. Religious life, therefore, has a mission to be fulfilled in a profound renewal of faith and spirituality. Religious women and men will themselves be the first to benefit from fidelity to this task.

2. That religious life be based on an extraordinary experience of Christ and that it give vitality to that experience

Religious life and mission will be inseparable and will result from a personal relationship with Jesus. The religious of the future will need to walk decisively in an encounter with the gospel in order to be a page of the gospel.

Each institute offers diverse ways, and sometimes creates a way, of entering into an intensive affective relationship with Christ in order to become transformed in and with Christ. Founders of religious institutes were persons who had an extraordinary experience with Jesus, a spiritual, mystical experience that developed into a deep attraction toward God, radical and almost irresistible, from which a new love was born. These founders' particular way of approaching Christ, of being conformed to the image of God's Son (see Rom 8:29), was the heart of their personal charism and became embodied in their institutes. The apostolic work, the mission, the giving of self to others, germinated from this experience and nourished it. The history of an institute is made by persons who are involved in this experience of Christ, which they assimilate and then transmit.

3. That the charismatic element of religious life be emphasized

Religious life is a charism (*Lumen Gentium* 43; *Perfectae Caritatis* 1), and when it is lived, the Christian is marked with all the notes of that charism: power, creativity, newness, spirituality, daring, availability, risk of the enterprise, service, and listening. When the religious life is faithful to its true spirit, it is capable of making all that is contrary to its charismatic power disappear: fear, routine, lukewarmness, insecurity, and uncertainty. The future must require of religious life a greater consciousness of, and connaturality with, its charismatic audacity. There are words and gestures that if not said and done by religious will remain unheard and unseen. The more perceptible the charismatic element of religious life becomes, the more attractive will religious life be to the youth of our time.

4. That religious institutes be identified as religious families

Religious life must typify and symbolize the family/community nature of Christian life. This will become an existential and concrete project inspired by the life and legislation of the founder and will mean that a family environment will characterize the religious group, marking its form of life as well as the style in which it carries out its apostolic activities. This family/community nature will give a determinative quality to religious consecration and mission.

This understanding of oneself as part of a family is not something exclusive to religious. It is, rather, an understanding shared by all believers. Religious, by *living* it, move toward greater integration with the wider community of God's people. The religious family itself will desire that it be extended to include both religious and laypeople. These various integrations, which will enrich religious life, will be expressed within the context of family life, in the sociopolitical enterprise, and in the physical work that religious undertake.

The spiritual family is the adequate ecclesial place in which religious can live and transmit the spiritual heritage of their founder. Such a religious family will hand on a spirit, a family environment, a tradition, an organization, and proposals for the future. All these will form and confirm vocations to religious life.

5. That religious life be continually more available to serve those who suffer injustice

There is no serious consecrated religious life if there is no listening to the clamor of the poor. Genuine religious life requires a keen conscience that responds to injustice. It must be marked by an urgency that the transformation of the world be accomplished by faith and the power of love. Our rediscovered awareness of injustice must cause us to question our apostolic service and our consecration.

6. That religious life continue and be lived in fullness, consciously linked with the dynamism of the Church

Religious must have an increasingly greater consciousness of belonging to the mystery and dynamism of the Church. We, as religious, are born for the vigorous impulse of the Holy Spirit in the heart of the Church. Religious are a sacrament of the Spirit's life and sanctity—a visible sign of the Church.

The dynamism of religious life tends to radicalize, to go beyond, to give from the members' own poverty, to be out-going, and, from its frontier, to reach toward the least evangelized. Its dynamism presupposes a cultural, geographical, and religious exodus, one that carries the religious to a strange land where itinerant poverty is experienced and where life is lived provisionally.

The witness of religious life in the Church must include reference to contemplation. Religious must give living testimony that the Christian life will be a more radical enterprise depending upon the extent to which such a life is involved with contemplation. Religious must accompany and assist other Christians to deepen their faith and their personal prayer. They must also offer to others their particular community spirit, and they must urge the Church to achieve solidarity with people who are suffering. All of this will help the people of God understand their own prophetic dimension, one that is expressed in a witness to spiritual and transcendent values.

* * *

Religious life will not move into the future by itself. Committed persons must take up this task. To whom shall we look as having a significant role in helping bring religious life into the next century? I suggest that we focus attention on the following:

1. The experience of religious life in Latin America, Africa, and Asia

The Church is currently trying to move from being culturally monocentric to being polycentric, as it attempts to leave its European style and take on a worldwide character. These ecclesial changes of perspective will, of course, affect religious life. Religious institutes are receiving more members in places such as Africa and Asia than in places where Christianity has had a long tradition; this fruitfulness will grow as both Christianity and religious life become more firmly established. There is no doubt that religious life in these countries will take on characteristic lines and features, some of which will mark religious life within the whole of the Church. New features are already sprouting in those places where religious have become profoundly rooted in the local culture and Church. The challenge that comes from dialogue with the sociopolitical reality is already contributing an original and strong expression to religious life in these places. The action of the Holy Spirit that blows where it will nourishes and sustains this creativity.

2. Religious communities inserted in the midst of people who are poor

It is important to draw attention to what is happening on the periphery, where religious communities are inserted in the midst of people who are poor. This style of life brings originality. While there is no doubt that "inserted" religious life is opening doors, such a way of living the religious life is not yet customary. Nevertheless, this form of life is a valid direction. Such a style of life originates in a spiritual experience; it continues and is sustained by that experience as well as by efforts to develop a spirituality consonant with it. This is an incarnational spirituality; those who have been awakened to it are not attempting to "add" something to religious life.

Rather, they have found within themselves a capacity to discover the face of God as God wants to be revealed, in human flesh, in the incarnation. These religious are particularly drawn to see and to be with God, as God is revealed in those who are poor and who live in places where living conditions are undeveloped. This option has profound ecclesial and biblical roots.

3. The religious young adult

Young people will themselves bring back the return of youth to religious life because they have an appreciation of the values of religious life, namely, prayer, community life, and insertion in the life of the Church. It is through the older members, however, that these young religious will be led to an intimate religious experience and will become mirrors of the wisdom of the interior life. It will be evident that they have received this personalized formation from the older religious. Only through such personal guidance will young people enter religious life and remain. It will be the task of those guiding religious formation to open to youth, with their initial generosity, horizons of interior life that would never occur to them spontaneously.

4. Directors of formation

It will be the formation directors who will have the task of giving form to the entire program of the renewal of religious life. In them we will need to find the spiritual dispositions that reveal a readiness to give testimony, to animate, and to confirm others in their vocations. These dispositions of a teacher are not acquired in the schools but in the desert and in the practice of "walking with" another person.

5. Religious women

An important task of women in the Church and in religious life will be to make feminine values strongly present. It will be because of women, for the most part, that the structures of religious life as well as of the Church will express all the richness of a redeemed femininity. Women will make less abstract the transmission of the evangelical message.

*   *   *

There is no doubt that religious life will continue to be *the* ecclesiastical place where the great challenges of Christians will be known. Pope John Paul II has said that upon us, the religious, depends, in great measure, the fortune of the Church. Because of this, religious life must continue to give concrete expression to gospel values and not become lost in speculation. This is not a call to triumphalism but rather a call to incarnation.

Religious life has a duty to put down roots wherever it exists. It is the religious who must offer soul, warmth, spirit, light: the transparency of the gospel. For this, neither strict silence nor complicated explanations are any good; rather, what is needed are sharing and giving. We are called to do all things continually from within, imitating the fecundity of Mary (Puebla 287–88). There is a metaphor in oriental wisdom that expresses this well: "See that window. It is just a hole in the wall, but thanks to that hole, the room is full of light." The religious of today will be faithful in their contribution to the Church and the world if they allow themselves to let the light of the Lord shine on society. The conviction is that this light will be a ferment, transforming the crowd into a town and the town into the people of God. This will be the realization of the hopes of Vatican II. The future, fervently desired, begins now. We place this future in the hands of God.

*   *   *

1. The religious life is above all an ecclesial event, an evangelical "praxis" that the spirit of Jesus has been sustaining in the history of the Church.
2. The religious life always carries within it the danger of installing itself in the center of power and security, thereby losing its religious identity.
3. The religious life has been called to return to its evangelical, charismatic origin.
4. Vatican Council II has manifested in its theology of religious life that religious life is a charism, a radical following of Jesus and a sign of the kingdom of God.
5. The theology of the First World emphasizes the transcendent character of religious life in a secular world, while the theology of the Third World, particularly in Latin America, emphasizes the prophetic dimension of religious life in an unjust world.
6. In Latin America, after Medellin and Puebla, many religious have inserted themselves in the midst of the people, making an exodus to the poor who are on the periphery of society.
7. The more that religious are open to a contemplative dimension, the more attentive they will be to the exigencies of the kingdom.
8. Our future will depend on the service that we, according to our charism, are capable of lending to the Church and to the world as we live the gospel.
9. Religious must live as participants in the historical experience of their own time.
10. A family environment is needed if we are to be in communion with the laity and with the poor.
11. To consider the course to be taken in the religious life we shall have to follow a double principle: incarnation and vigilance.
12. The religious life must be based on an extraordinary experience of Christ.

13. Through discernment and audacity, religious life will attain a harmonious synthesis that will make simple and vital its presence in the world.
14. The future of the religious life and of religious institutes are in the hands of God.

Bibliography

1. Arnáiz, José María and José María Guerrero, *Caminos de Futuro de la Vida Religiosa* (Madrid: Instituto teológico de vida religiosa, 1987).

2. Castaño, Jorge Iván, *La Vida Religiosa en Puebla Desafíos* (Bogotá: Ediciones Paulinas, 1980).

3. Codina, Víctor and Noé Zevallos, *Vida Religiosa Historia y Teología*, (Bogotá: Ediciones Paulinas, 1984).

4. III Conferencia General del Episcopado Latinoamericano. *Puebla* (Venezuela: Ediciones Tripode, 1979).

5. *Nuevos Horizontes de la Vida Religiosa* (Bogotá: Ediciones Paulinas, 1984).

Part II

Where We Have Come From and Where We Now Stand

The breadth and depth of her far-reaching mind and experience are apparent in this paper by Mary L. O'Hara, C.S.J., professor of philosophy at the College of Saint Mary in Omaha, Nebraska. In looking toward the future of religious life Sister Mary reminds us to listen carefully to our own experience, which gives rise to questions that must be addressed with wisdom, with a "sapiential habit of mind" that looks at the whole picture of reality including its major component, mystery. Especially thought provoking is Sister Mary's example of the "road not taken" by religious communities in the early 1960s and the consequences that might have resulted for the future had that road been taken. After naming some areas where religious might direct their future efforts—involvement with the new immigrants, "hedge schools," dialogue with nuns of other cultures and beliefs—Sister Mary speaks of the need to establish a center where systematic studies of issues connected with the future of religious life can be carried on.

3

Heralds of Hope

Mary L. O'Hara, C.S.J.

Since there is one thing we know for sure about the future, that it is uncertain in most respects, what we shall need to do in planning for it is to remain aware that we must always regard our findings as tentative, at least in their relation to other data. It belongs to the sciences to investigate, each in its own area, the data available to research. Between the presently cultivated scientific fields, however, there may always be an uncultivated field, still to be discovered, which, somewhat like an undiscovered planet, may introduce an unexplained bias into our otherwise orderly universe of discourse. We need the sapiential habit of mind to keep us humble enough to recognize the limits of our present knowledge.

Wisdom in the Modern Age

Notably absent from the contemporary world is any mention of the intellectual virtue of wisdom. Identified in ancient times by Aristotle as the highest good habit of the mind, wisdom was held in the greatest esteem by St. Thomas Aquinas and many other ancient and medieval thinkers. If such a mental habit is indeed possible for human beings, it must be of capital importance for every human enterprise, including that of religious life.

What is wisdom? For Aristotle it is the knowledge of all things in their highest causes, and it therefore enables one who

35

possesses it to judge and order all things. It differs from the sciences, with their limited areas of interest, in being concerned with everything. It goes beyond science not only in the number of things with which it is concerned but also in that it is able to defend scientific assumptions: the axioms of geometry, for example, which are not defended within the science itself. Thus wisdom may include the realm of what science does not grasp, as well as science itself.

Science in our modern sense was actually a Greek, largely an Aristotelian, invention, although it is only in modern times that it has come into its own and achieved astounding successes. With the coming of modern times, however, even the word "wisdom" came to be less used, and when it was used, it most often referred to what Aristotle called "prudence," which he defined as ". . . a disposition for action concerning what is good or bad for man. . . ."[1] It referred, that is, to the good sense a person needs to live effectively in the world, to get ahead.

Ironically, it was Logical Positivists in the twentieth century who helped to show, in their excessive desire to make logical science the ruling kind of knowledge, that there is in fact a place for wisdom above science, when their project came to be seen as logically impossible. The arid Logical Positivist approach ill prepared Westerners for the large-scale encounters with the East that followed the beginning of the Second World War.

Gabriel Marcel, on the other hand, emphasizes the need for human beings to learn to live with mystery, and not to reduce mysteries to (scientific) problems to be solved. It is the place of wisdom to do this. It seems to me that what we need to do is to confront the sapiential reality, the wisdom component of human life today. This is where the greatest challenges of our age are found: in ecology, for example, or in the realm of medical, business, and communications ethics, wherever it is necessary to include in the equation that most important and mysterious element, the human person.

It is a question of seeing things in relation to the greatest reality, ultimately to God. Marx rejected this way of looking at things; other modern thinkers neglected it. The crumbling of communist societies today invites us to try to build a new society in which mystery and wisdom will be at home. We suffer today from having lost knowledge in our pursuit of information, wisdom in pursuing knowledge, as T.S. Eliot has pointed out.

To be able to formulate a question in such a way as to know how to get the answer is itself a considerable accomplishment. This is the business of science. But beyond the clearly formulated problem lies the penumbra of mystery, the realm of prayer, of communion with God and with one another. If we lose sight of this whole vision of reality, we condemn ourselves to partial and conflicting solutions, to the sorts of endless battles we are now involved in, such as the controversy about acid rain.

Here is where the difficult questions emerge first. Here is where we need to try to discern what it is that we desire to address, how to formulate in researchable chunks, as it were, the amorphous mass of experience as it develops day by day. Only those who are actually experiencing the form of life that gives rise to the questions are in a position finally to say that the questions have been thoroughly and validly addressed, as Wittgenstein has taught us.

Here is where we need, therefore, to listen carefully to our own experience and to try to discern what it is that the Lord is calling us to in the future.

The Road Not Taken

The philosopher Heidegger says somewhere that guilt follows upon a decision to take one course of action rather than another, apparently regardless of whether the choice is a wise one or not; the sense of having closed off paths we might have pursued leaves us feeling we have not accomplished what we might have. Without wanting to inflict feelings of guilt, I invite you to think for a moment about a "road not taken" by the American Church some thirty years ago.

That was when Pope John XXIII, that astonishing man, made one of his many hard to understand but perhaps graced and surely intuitive suggestions. He asked American religious to send ten percent of their members to Latin America. How the decision to ignore this idea was taken by those superiors who did not accept it, I am not sure; one or two major superiors whom I asked about it at the time said it was simply impossible; we could never spare so many people. (We all know we have spared many times that number since.) And when I have tried recently to introduce the question of what happened then, I have been told not to "load guilt" upon people.

I repeat that I don't intend to load guilt, but it seems to me clear that there is an interesting and possibly important lesson here for us today. And so I intend to pursue some musings regarding time and place: How might things be different today had we been there then?

What if our superiors in the early sixties had decided against the counsels of human prudence and sent sisters and brothers in very large numbers to assist in Latin America? What would the effects have been here? And there?

My guess is that one of the first things that would have happened would have been the uncoupling of religious from the institutions they were for the most part employed in at that time. What has since taken place—the turning over of institutions to predominantly lay staffs—would have happened earlier, and in an atmosphere of realistic coming to terms with the demands of the extraordinary situation of the missionary call. Withdrawal of religious from schools, an action interpreted by some as willfulness on the part of religious when it happened five years later, might have been seen by lay parishioners as a joint sacrifice they and the sisters and brothers were required to make. In any case, the suburban schools that might have been left unstaffed by religious would have been able, economically, to continue to function without the sisters' and brothers' subsidy, and lay men and women might have assumed the necessary leadership five years earlier than they in fact began to assume it.

What might have been the effect on the large numbers of talented young women and men then receiving their religious training? Instead of being destined for one of a few schools operated by a religious community, they might have found themselves in a Third World situation in which matters of life and death instead of campus politics were everyday affairs. In those relatively cloistered days we rarely came into contact with religious of other communities even in our own city. In the foreign setting a much broader sharing would have been the usual practice.

What might have been the effect on Latin America? It is hard to say, given the speed with which events have moved there.

The Road Taken—And Some of Its Problems

Within a recent twenty-four-hour period of time I received two impressions of what some people may see as religious life today. At a charismatic meeting the principal speaker said to me, "Religious life is in a very bad way today"; and then he mentioned a community well known to me and said, "and they are the worst off of all."

The following day I saw a performance of the play *The House of Blue Leaves* by John Guare, in which three zany nuns are portrayed as cheerily breaking one after another of their vows with no sign of any remorse. At the end, two are killed in an explosion and the third leaves the order. The audience feels no sympathy for any of them; they are portrayed as decidedly unpleasant characters. And their faults are not merely individual idiosyncracies; they grow out of the very institutional setting of their lives. One goes uninvited to the cupboard of an apartment they have happened into and seizes a jar of peanut butter, saying, "We never have this in the convent!"

I received the first of these impressions in the deeply serious atmosphere of a meeting of Catholic charismatics, where many persons were "slain in the Spirit" and where there was a frequent murmur of strange tongues. The second might have been found amusing in a very sophisticated setting in which its sardonic bite could be appreciated. (The audience in which I saw it received the nuns' performance in total silence.)

We who see religious life from the inside, as the life we have lived for many years, see both these views of our life as inauthentic; they are nevertheless portrayals of our way of living today (or in the recent past; the play is set at the time of Pope Paul VI's visit to New York, and the nuns are in the old habits) that are seen by thousands of people and perhaps assumed by many of them to be true.

We have come, in my time in religious life, from a period when, in an upper-middle-class neighborhood in Brussels, my sister companion and I had a dog sicked on us by people we did not know, a situation in which I think it was not our American but our religious character that was being insulted. And we have come to a position in which our life is interpreted to the general public through the mass media, whether the stereotype be Mother Teresa or the Flying Nun. Somewhere in between, while Kennedy was president, we probably enjoyed a certain vogue, which, however, did not necessarily mean that we were better understood.

Image and reality. How do we bring them together? How make the image more authentic? (Tim Unsworth has written accurately and perceptively in the *National Catholic Reporter* about the silly images of both men and women religious in the mass media.) One way to do it is by letting the public see us as we really are, as occasionally they do, when, for example, nuns and priests were seen in the front ranks of the crowds bringing about the People Power revolution in the Philippines.

We are understandably somewhat shy about letting our light shine, even though we know the Gospel imperative. For one thing, the starkness of our lives can at times be frightening: the average age of sisters in my own province, for example, is about seventy—a tribute to the advance of medicine since the days when sisters died within five years of entering, as we can see when we visit the old cemeteries, but scary in the palpable emptiness of our large buildings and the rarity of the uncontrolled laughter of youth in our houses.

My second grade teacher, Helen Dolores Sweeney, C.S.J., wrote of her feelings as she saw the thinning of the ranks, as her friends died before her:

> Run, sheep, run—
> And You're the One
> Who breaks the rules:
> You lead us all a tortuous chase
> And then you hide, and run,
>   and run, and hide.
> The daylight turns to dusk
> And then to dark
> And I'm the only sheep now running in
>   this race.
> All others
> You have taken home.
>
> Yes, one by one
> The rustlings
> And the sounds of running feet
> Have ceased:

The calls, the shrieks, the signals and
    the shouts
All fade away
Until the echo of my voice
Is all I hear.

O everlasting Prey,
Will you or I be caught?
Which is the seeker—
Which the sought?
Your running is so silent and so fleet,
And I grow clumsy, weary
And uncertain in the race.
When will you call to me,
"O run, sheep, run!"
And guide me safely home?

—For My Friends, Home Safe
April 21, 1982

Is there any of us who has not felt a sinking feeling as we listened for the rustlings, the sounds of running feet, the calls, the shrieks, the signals and the shouts and heard instead only the echo of our own voice?[2]

A Mysterious Calling

The principal obstacle to an understanding of our way of life, however, is the fact that it is fundamentally a mystery. It goes against the mainstream of every dominant culture; our celibacy guarantees that.

So does our obedience. I remember a superior general who rebuked me for not blindly obeying the Church's regulation on abstinence when I ate meat, as I took it to be, on Friday. Everyone was obviously enjoying the steak, all of them my elders and several my superiors, and talking about the fact that it was Friday. I found this surprising, but since they were all doing it (I had been in the kitchen when the conversation started, and so had not heard the beginning of it), I fell to with a very good will and enjoyed it immensely, finding out only later that it was whale steak and permitted on Friday. She found my behavior unedifying; I found her disapproval silly: why would I question the action of my superiors on a matter of such grave importance? I had assumed we must have some special permission.

I still remember where I was standing at the bulletin board in our community room when in May 1945 I read Dorothy Thompson's first *Life* report on the Nazi concentration camps. I had heard rumors from my teachers, some of them refugees from Hitler's Germany, of dreadful atrocities committed against the Jews; but I had discounted them as propaganda. What could not be gainsaid were the pictures of living skeletons piled one on top of another in the death camps. This, with Eichmann's trial later, when he defended himself as ''doing what he was told,'' made me see the sort of blind obedience my superior seemed to be calling for in the matter of the steak as never again suitable for life in our world. Our obedience, our listening for the voice of God in our lives, must occur in the context of the human situation, not simply as a rote response to the letter of the law. Religious can perhaps model a new understanding of obedience for the larger society, one young people can appreciate. Much of the tragedy of the drug epidemic in our time might have been avoided had children obeyed their parents and teachers in this matter.

Not only obedience, however, but the other vows and virtues have needed updating. The ancient philosopher Plotinus has this to say about the union of soul and body (*Enneads*, I, 2):

> Since the soul is evil when it is thoroughly mixed with the body and shares its experiences and has all the same opinions, it will be good and possess virtue when it no longer has the same opin-

ions but acts alone—this is intelligence and wisdom—and does not share the body's experiences—this is self-control . . . (Loeb).

What Plotinus has to say here reminds me of some of the novitiate teachings and retreat preaching on the vow and virtue of chastity: the ideal, it seemed, was to be without a body, or to act as though one had no body. A strong stoic and Neoplatonic strain has characterized Christian piety throughout much of its history.[3] We surely need to bring our more balanced understanding of the whole human being today to bear upon our expressions of spiritual life, including the life of vowed celibacy for the love of God.[4]

One of the reasons for the small number of young people in our religious communities is no doubt the unflattering picture of religious life presented in the media. Another is the lack of acceptance by young people today of the value of commitment to anything, least of all to a "state" of life, including the married state. The very idea of "stasis" in a changing world sounds rather absurd if not dangerous: think of clinging to a pylon as you are being swept along by a raging current.

Religious men and women, as they face problems connected with aging, may serve as a sort of pilot group for other segments of the population. While the population of the United States has increased in absolute terms, there are fewer young people in proportion to the rest of the population than there were a generation or two ago. The entire nation faces a problem of dealing with a growing group of aging persons while supporting these individuals on a shrinking base of younger employed men and women. In my own province today, there is no one under thirty years of age.

New Hedge Schools?

Former Secretary of Education Bennett, while in office, challenged parochial schools to take in persons who have dropped out of public schools and others who have not been reached by the usual educational methods and to educate them. In the same article in which Bennett's speech (to the spring 1988 convention of the National Catholic Education Association) was reported, there was the familiar reaction of a member of the education establishment: separation of Church and State would make such a project impossible.

But what if religious men and women set up nonreligious learning centers in which such persons could be taught? What if the old Irish "hedge schools" (in one of which my great-grandfather learned to read, in defiance of the oppressive laws then enforced by the English) were to be revived for the benefit of the children of homeless people whose transient status keeps them from enrolling in schools in the public system? Our poverty has for decades made it easy for us to identify with the poor, to reach them, to help them in practical ways. This new opportunity presents us with a possible way of helping the new poor of our time. Whether or not this project can be realized, there is clearly work out there for religious, and even for the older religious who are still able to be active, though no longer perhaps in a conventional classroom. In fact, the question of the employment of older religious is a pressing one. Recently a Taiwanese monsignor, vicar general of his diocese, invited me to come with two other sisters to establish a junior college in Taiwan. When I said, "But our sisters are old," he said, "That doesn't make any difference."

Fortunately this question is beginning to be addressed by projects such as ENCOR in Cincinnati, aimed at employing older but still active religious. It is to be hoped that as such projects as these take hold, we religious will be able to spark some self-help projects among older laypersons, for example, telephone apostolates.

Hegel treats much of life in terms of dialectic, of the opposing forces that call out for synthesis; Marx translated this, oversimply, into class warfare. But when we begin to speak of American Catholics, it is important that we recognize that our entire history, at least until very recently, has been one of dialectical relationship with Protestants. It was to the Protestants that the public schools effectively belonged in the early days, at least in the Midwest—less so in heavily Catholic centers like Boston where an entire classroom, teacher and all, might be Catholic in a public school. In a society dominated by the constant push of the Protestant work ethic and the shrewdness of Protestant use of wealth, Catholics were for the whole of the nineteenth century obliged to look first at the conservation of very meager Church resources. Little wonder that both bishops and religious superiors were often administrators and only then pastoral figures.

In those difficult and precarious times, it is not to be wondered at if the interest of the Church (e.g., to present a united front, etc.) was seen to amount to the same thing as the male interest. So it was that when St. Louis University in the thirties became perhaps the first Jesuit school to admit women, the neighboring women's colleges were not heard to protest loudly at the injustice of having their "natural" constituencies skimmed off by the new coeducational arrangement that would eventually, there and in other places throughout the country, cause their demise as Catholic women's colleges, or would lead to their seeking further differentiation (for example, in the recent case of my own alma mater, by establishing a Weekend College to appeal to working women). What seemed to the comptrollers of the men's colleges (usually larger, not always better, than the women's colleges) their manifest destiny certainly helped make their financial statements look better. And the women generally uttered no public protest; we swallowed the looting of our hard-won constituencies without a murmur and started over in some different field.

I don't know whether this was a wise way to practice poverty and obedience; but it was not likely to be one that appealed to young women. And the women who in the past might have been attracted to religious life by a college teacher's example would often in the new situation not meet a religious woman in this setting, and would assume that all religious were active on the grade or high school level, an occupation not necessarily appealing to upwardly mobile young persons.

Evidently this sort of thing has had its effect upon religious communities' finances. Religious women have had to be exceedingly agile to get around the sudden contraction in demands for their services that has followed upon such actions as the "going coed" of traditionally men's schools. (The current crisis in retirement funds for religious might seem to call for a moratorium on the further alienation of common property, that is, the turning over to secular use and ownership, without compensation, the buildings and land the communities have acquired over many years.)

One response of women religious has been to turn to active social work at the level of those marginalized by our society: battered women, the homeless, and similar groups. What we are finding is that our vow of poverty is being lived out in a different way from what it might have been forty years ago.

Still, it is evident from the examples given above that there remains, at least potentially, a serious morale problem for those of us who have chosen to remain religious in these difficult times. How do I as a religious respond to the unspoken or explicit questions of family members or friends about religious life as they perceive it portrayed in the media or in certain religious groups like that of the charismatic leader I mentioned above?

I shall not attempt just now to answer this question. Instead I shall undertake to talk about the basis for all our life, the hope that has been our anchor as religious but first of all as baptized members of Christ.

The Source of All Our Hope

Easter Sunday this year in Omaha was foggy. As I looked at the stained glass windows in the Poor Clare chapel, I was struck by the fact that the cooler colors, the blues and greens, predominated, with the reds and oranges and yellows hardly any brighter than the blues. When the sun is bright, the reds come forward in such a way that one could at times be persuaded the windows were eight inches thick.

The windows are an apt image of the way in which religious life can appear to us who live it today: the disquieting demographic statistics are not to be gainsaid, the sociological and psychological findings that make religious life seem improbable if not impossible are not easily dismissed; but the bright little light of faith is, in the end, what makes our life comprehensible to us when we are able to see it in that way.

The Place and Time That Is Ours

All of us Christians live under a "sacred canopy" that stretches from the East to the lands of sunset here in the West.[5] The bright sunrise can perhaps already be seen in the Orient and in the Southern Hemisphere. It will take a while for things to become equally clear for us here. But we do wait in joyful hope for the coming of our Savior who will make the meaning of our lives plain to us. St. Thérèse of Lisieux already prepared us for this present time of darkness when in her own life she looked at an iron curtain when she tried to lift her eyes to heaven.

We have, most of us, been born into a world which to many people seems to have been providentially preserved from the course of Oriental and European civilization for millenia. Our forebears had few scruples about pushing the Native American population back in their pursuit of a manifest destiny that has for the most part been realized. This is the background for our self-understanding: we are Americans, though the precise meaning of this reality is an ever-changing one. A constant feature of American life, however, has been the sometimes grudging but always repeated welcoming of new peoples into our midst.

Repeatedly the immigrant population has been the salvation of the nation as a whole. It was to this immigrant population that the religious men and women, a century or more ago, ministered in a variety of ways. It was a ministry of like to like: a member of the newly arrived group would join an order in which she would, after her initial training period, be sent back into the group from which she had come to educate other members and perhaps attract some of them into the religious life.

A very few of our more prophetic members have in the face of the recent immigration from Southeast Asia reached out to these newcomers, frequently not Christians. Most of us have been too occupied with the daily demands of ministry in already established institutions to find the time for these new undertakings. Yet it is very likely that from these relatively younger populations, future vocations may come. Similarly, a color barrier persists in that few of us come into frequent social contact with our Black brothers and sisters. Here again, however, is a likely source of future religious—despite the cultural barriers that exist.

Ours is a privileged place, to many of us a holy place. Nowhere since the Tower of Babel has there been such an assemblage of different voices. It is important, it seems to me, that we religious attune our ears to them; but for most of us, this is an unfinished task, if not one yet to be begun.

In the five hundred years since Columbus, the two continents of the Americas have treated the Native American inhabitants differently. In Canada, treaties were made and apparently respected. Here, as repeated lawsuits even today attest, it was trickery and arrogance that the Native American frequently met at the hands of the white newcomer. In Latin America, intermarriage or at least a *modus vivendi* was frequently established. To this continent were brought Africans pressed into slavery, to the number of some ten percent of the population. The majority of our ancestors played a part, actively or collaboratively, in these events, or simply as passive spectators who had trouble keeping alive themselves.

Recent return to the founder's vision and search for the charism proper to each religious group, mandated by Vatican II, have resulted in keen realization that much that had been treated in recent years as important for the life of a religious was in reality irrelevant or even inimical to the original ideals of the founder—or perhaps even to the fundamental tenets of Christianity. The substitution of human regulations and their observance for charity and intimate life with God was found to be killing to the human spirit, which is the sole means of making religious values actually living. For religious, this often meant that those who most exactly tried to observe the laws and accepted observances were, as a direct result, the least prepared to weather the storm unleashed by Vatican II.

Other Cultures

But Vatican Council II spoke principally to Catholics. What of other women and men of other religious traditions throughout the world? In the course of visits with many religious women in other parts of the world—women who professed various beliefs while sharing the common note of living as nuns—I was profoundly impressed by the sincerity of their commitment to their chosen way of life and their openness and willingness to share with someone who came to them from a very different world.

Is it not imperative for us to begin now to think about ways in which we can draw closer to these women of very different

outlook and background and belief from our own, Hindus and
Buddhists and Jains as well as our Christian separated brothers
and sisters who adopt a vowed way of life?

On the banks of the sacred Cauvery River, opposite and
a few miles distant from Fr. Bede Griffiths' ashram, I met a
Hindu nun. She told me how she came to religious life, an un-
usual development in Hinduism, which traditionally knows
of individual ascetics but apparently not of communities committed to a lifetime of celibacy. Her brother had told her of a
new group forming under the headship of a guru. Although
her parents were very much opposed to her following this
mode of life, her brother helped her to accomplish her purpose and join the group. Now they operate a school for girls,
occasionally undertake a pilgrimage to some shrine, and provide an opportunity for Westerners to learn yoga and Sanskrit.
She has been a member of the group of some twenty to thirty
women for thirty years. One of their number lives as a hermit. She indicated that she would like to get in touch with other
interested religious women.

In Japan and Korea I visited Buddhist nuns who are, like
the Hindus, non-Christians; but unlike the Hindu women,
Buddhists have a tradition of women ascetics going back to
the time of Christ. This ancient form of life has many different
manifestations: Japanese nuns serve as priests in temples,
while those of Sri Lanka are denied this opportunity. Still, all
are inspired by the teachings of the Buddha, all try to practice
the tenets of Buddhism. And although the Japanese parliament
has permitted Buddhist men priests to marry in this century,
the women with whom I talked value their celibacy and have
no intention of abandoning it. I received an impression, in-
cidentally, of a possible conflict arising between the wife of a
married priest and a nun serving as a priest.

In Japan, the monastery in which I stayed was a kind of
seminary for women priests. In Korea I met a woman appar-

ently in a kind of apprentice relationship with a married male Buddhist priest.

In the course of seeking out someone among the Jain nuns of India with whom I could talk philosophy, I met many women of various disciplines: Digambara, Swetambara, both idolatrous and non-idolatrous. These women have a tradition even more ancient than that of the Buddhists: there are historical records of Jain nuns going back to 500 B.C. They are peripatetic, having no fixed abode, no monasteries or convents. Simply to find them, therefore, presents a problem. Except during the rainy season (a variable time for different years and different parts of India), these women walk barefoot from one village to another, remaining no more than two or three days in each place, preaching to the people and receiving from them their daily meals. In this way the people are able to have some experience of the divine, since the only way in which God exists, for Jains, is in these ascetics, whose lives of strenuous endeavor finally will enable them to escape from an otherwise endless cycle of rebirth into a life of complete knowledge and endless bliss.

I found most of these women urbane and welcoming, though initially somewhat surprised that a Catholic nun should want to find out something about their life. Few, however, spoke English. Very often a young Jain laywoman who happened to be present (the nuns were nearly always surrounded by visitors) would help interpret. Frequently these women had learned their English in convent schools.

These Jain ascetics had questions to ask me. They are interested in Catholic nuns, but I gather they have little opportunity to meet them. More than once I heard an Indian Catholic religious say: "I have lived here for many years and I knew nothing of the Jain nuns' existence in these parts!"

In Israel, Greece, and Egypt I met and talked with Coptic and Orthodox nuns as well as Byzantine rite Catholic nuns.

Here again, language was a barrier. And once again, as with the non-Christian nuns, I felt the need to enter into the symbolism that was so important to them.

My contact with these women religious has made me aware of the need for closer ties among religious women throughout the world. Desiderata for this work include:

- a speaking and reading knowledge of the pertinent languages, e.g., Japanese, Korean, Hindi, Arabic, Greek;
- an understanding of the important symbols proper to each group. "The broom is the most important," said a Jain nun, because it symbolizes the vow of nonviolence, in sweeping out of one's way the smallest insect that might otherwise be harmed.
- openness to learn, and some education in the traditions of the various groups;
- willingness to adapt to customs usual in these groups, e.g., vegetarianism, manner of sitting;
- willingness and ability to articulate our own tradition so that it is understandable to other women;
- willingness to receive them into our own setting (community) to the extent possible.

Need for a Center to Study the Future of Religious Life

Most of all, however, my experience convinces me that we need to establish a center where systematic studies of issues connected with the future (and thus also the past and the present) of religious life can be carried on. To such a center interested persons could come to exchange ideas and results of research and to discuss with others ideas for further research. Such questions as the kinds of law governing each group and the origin of the laws and their effect on the lives of the nuns are some of the many matters that need to be addressed.

If it is objected that there is no need for such a center, I would ask where this work is now being done. Where can persons interested in pursuing such research go to get expert help in preparing for it? Where can studies in intercultural understanding take place, not only occasionally but on a continuing basis? There is need for a recognized international center to which data pertinent to the entire question can be referred and in which one interested in this question can hope to find the best available research strategies being used. Questions that fall between the cracks of current research could be entertained in such a center, and ways found to address them. Finally, we need a center in which religious themselves will be able to bring to the surface from their experience the questions central to the preservation of the most important values of religious life.

As we emerge from the cloister of our own culture-bound experience and expectations, we need to prepare ourselves for meetings that will inevitably occur as the world becomes smaller, to prepare for the challenge of the future in ways that are mutually encouraging and enlightening.

From my travels in Israel I preserve a humiliating and illuminating picture: of myself somehow having wandered into a cul-de-sac in a rugged wadi where the only way out was up a six-foot sheer rock. Several Maryknoll priests and brothers clambered up the steep slope and pushed and pulled me, with failing heart, over the top, a Jesuit giving the final heave. As I thought about my predicament on the way back to our tour bus, I realized what a disaster it could have been, and not for me alone but for the entire group, if I had suffered a broken ankle and the bus had been miles instead of yards away. It seemed to me an image of our life as religious: we have perhaps in the past taken aboard persons who were rather poor risks for the rugged reality of religious life. In the present age of reassessment, these are people hunkered down avoiding the disturbing questions I have raised in this paper.

How is it then, that I can speak of hope in our present situation? Aristotle tells us hope is associated with a mental picture of what keeps us safe (*Rhetoric* 1383a17–20). As we look at the Jain nuns who have endured through two and a half millenia, can we doubt that religious life is a possible and needed alternative to the more general call of most people to married life? Perhaps we religious women and men can model hope, can be heralds of hope for those who see few signs of it in our present world. And as we Christians look at the majestic face of Christ in some of the great icons, can we doubt that we are kept safe by Jesus who has called us to come after him as he himself becomes present in this our rapidly changing time?

Plotinus characterized finite beings as the sort of beings who cannot exist if they have no future. Teilhard de Chardin has recently expressed a similar psychological need for human beings. For us religious especially, whose life has always been an eschatologically oriented one, it is both necessary and feasible to express our faith in the Lord who is to come by a firm and realistic hope in his love for us whom he has called by name to follow him.[6]

Notes

1. *Aristotle's Nicomachean Ethics,* trans. H. G. Apostle, VI, 5, 1140 b 5 (Grinnell, Iowa: The Peripatetic Press, 1984).

2. Marian Louwagie, C.S.J., has detailed many of the recent changes in religious life in her unpublished M.A. thesis, "The Emergence of a New Paradigm for the Sisters of St. Joseph, St. Paul Province" (The College of Saint Catherine, 1989).

3. See my "Truth in Spirit and Letter: Gregory the Great, Thomas Aquinas, and Maimonides on the Book of Job," in *From Cloister to Classroom,* ed. E. R. Elder (Kalamazoo: Cistercian Publications, 1986).

4. Michel Foucault's *A History of Sexuality,* vol 1 (New York: Pantheon Books, 1978) might be studied in relation to the question of the evolution of religious rules in the past century.

5. See Peter L. Berger, *The Sacred Canopy* (Garden City, N.Y.: Doubleday and Company, Inc., 1967.

6. See Rom 5:1-5.

*T*he future of religious communities is in its members, in actual persons who will be attracted to choose religious life. Making available the insights of thirty-five scholars, including herself, consulted by the Quinn Commission about the postconciliar decline in religious vocations, Mary Ewens, O.P., of the Cushwa Center for the Study of American Catholicism, University of Notre Dame, points here to factors within religious communities that bear on future membership. She invites religious to the "ministry of conversation," taking as an example Mary Ward and her sisters in seventeenth-century England. Among other things Sister Mary notes the importance of developing friendships with young adults and of sharing with them our life of intimacy with Christ, our joy and enthusiasm for our vocation, and a clear articulation of our identity and mission.

4

Lessons from the Quinn Consultation

Mary Ewens, O.P.

The pontifical commission established by Pope John Paul II in 1983 to study the state of religious life in America used several approaches to gather information that would inform their deliberations. Among them was the assembly of sociological data describing the decline in vocations since Vatican II. To aid in their understanding of the significance of that data, the members of the commission (Archbishops John Quinn and Thomas C. Kelly, O.P., and Bishop Raymond Lessard) asked thirty-five scholars from many fields, most of them religious, to write essays reacting to it from the vantage point of their own experience and expertise. These papers were then distributed to all of the writers for further comment and were discussed at a colloquium held in San Francisco.

Participation in this project was a grueling but stimulating experience. For one like myself, who had been involved in heavy administrative work for many years, it was like a crash course in the latest theories of psychosocial development, culture clash, theological and historical interpretation, change, and the research that has been done on many aspects of the call and response to a religious vocation. Particularly exciting was the fact that these scholars, working independently of one another in probing the reasons for the decline in vocations, arrived at similar conclusions. There was fairly broad agreement on major factors that affect the development of vocations.

It is not my task to discuss the complex findings of these essays here. They have been summarized in the December 4, 1986 issue of *Origins*, and sixteen of the papers have been published by Paulist Press in *The Crisis in Religious Vocations*, edited by Laurie Felknor. These are not papers of the Quinn Commission strictly speaking, but they did inform the group's deliberations. Though they focused on reasons why many left religious communities and few joined, they also contain insights which are useful for reflection by anyone concerned about the future of religious life. It is these that I would like to discuss in this essay.

Many of the factors which have affected the decline in vocations are cultural ones which are beyond the control of the Church and its religious communities. Some, however, are closely related to the living out of the commitment of individual members and communities. They are within the control of the groups themselves, and do impinge on future membership. Though the research on factors that influence vocations is probably familiar to formation personnel and community administrators, it deserves to be more widely known among all who are concerned about the future of religious life. Let us examine what these factors are and their implications for communities which hope to flourish into the future.

Several studies have shown that the most important human influence on the development of religious vocations comes from knowing well a sister, brother, or priest who is happy and fulfilled in religious life. This undisputed fact has serious implications which should be studied and discussed as communities ponder their mission and charism.

How does an unmarried young adult come to know a religious well today? The average age of entrants to communities is twenty-seven. How many people in their mid-twenties, who are making life commitments, are in contact with a sister, priest, or brother?

In earlier days sisters' communities often expressed as a motivation for opening high schools the fact that vocations would develop within them. Many communities had boarding schools which provided an easy and natural way for students to become familiar with religious and their lifestyle. Today most of those boarding schools have closed, and the percentage of religious in high schools has declined sharply. Catholic colleges should be a source of vocations, as should be also those who collaborate with religious in their work. Karen Kennelly, C.S.J., found, in her research on her St. Paul community, the Sisters of St. Joseph of Carondelet, that many who entered in the past already had relatives in the congregation.[1] Though families are smaller and less cohesive today, this should still be an area in which friendships with religious can flourish and the life be made known.

Ministries of many kinds could provide opportunities for contact with religious, but do they have the time, the leisure, to spend in developing a friendship or at least a friendly relationship? Religious today are harried with numerous demands on their time and energy. Psychiatrist James Tucker, S.S., finds that stress and burnout are the chief reasons that religious seek psychiatric counseling. As he notes, excessive workloads militate against the spending of time with young people who might become interested in a vocation.[2]

Of course, if young adults come to know sisters and priests but find them unhappy, disgruntled, complaining, or bitter they will not be attracted to their lifestyle. Job satisfaction is one of the chief causes for a feeling of happiness and self-worth in our society, says Tucker, and efforts to achieve that for all members should be an important goal for communities. Reasons for unhappiness and poor morale should be probed and attended to.

The essence of religious life, and the only reason which can justify embracing it, is a life of intimacy with Jesus Christ. Unfortunately, however, that is the last thing most religious would think of discussing with their communities, much less a young adult friend. As several writers of the Quinn consultation papers noted, we are very reluctant to talk about our deepest experiences of prayer and union with Christ. Yet how can we expect anyone to be drawn to this aspect of our life if it is not joyously shared with them?

How do we show potential recruits that we belong to a warm, supportive community which promotes friendship and bonding? Even where there is a healthy community life it is not easy to devise ways to draw others in to experience it. Because of the work pressures mentioned above, many groups find it difficult to set aside even one night a week when they can spend time with one another. To find time to relax and to share with others can be almost impossible.

And what impression will the visitor carry away of the spirit, mission, and identity of the group? Many communities, having gone through the turmoil of the years of renewal, are still groping for a clear sense of their new identity. Lack of a corporate identity that is a source of pride and focus for the members is a hindrance to recruitment. Who would be willing to cast their lot with a group that does not know who it is or where it is going? Some of the writers felt that it was important to have a mission aimed at peace and justice, individual challenge, and a countercultural stance. Flexibility, risk taking, and mobility, they felt, can mark the religious of the future, and they saw religious undertaking kinds of works that would be difficult for lay ministers, particularly married ones, to carry out. Empowering and collaborating with the laity were seen as other imperatives. ''Religious institutes will prosper,'' says James Hennesey, S.J., "when there is a real sense among God's people that collectively and individually, by the way they live and pray together and by the contribution they make to the commonweal, they respond to deeply felt needs within the Christian body."[3]

It is not enough to share the ordinary, humdrum aspects of our lives with young people. They have got to be shown the special moments, the satisfaction of helping others and of sharing their deepest aspirations, the joys and sorrows, if this life is to attract them. As psychiatrist James Gill, S.J., writes:

> Athletes can describe for the young the exciting victories they have won in the tense, final moments of crucial games. Actors can tell of moments filled with elation at the end of perform-ances. . . . Physicians can recall times of deep and lasting joy resulting from administering a surgical or medical treatment that saved a precious life heroically. The successful practitioners of other professions can create similarly appealing images for those who are thinking about following in their footsteps. But, I have found, when the practitioner is a priest or religious, the work life is often less excitingly described.[4]

Gill's essay presents a cogent development of this theme. The values that permeate American culture and engage the atten-tion of young adults are far more attractive than is their per-ception of the reality of religious life. Psychologist Donna Markham, O.P., found, in her research into the attitudes that various groups have toward religious life for women, that high school girls in schools run by sisters did not view sisters' lives positively. High school, college, and single women did not find them to be dynamic people. This leads Markham to take a pes-simistic view of the future prospects of religious life for women.[5]

Letting young people come to know our lives, and mak-ing sure that they see happy, holy religious living in suppor-tive communities is not enough. A surprising number of

recruits told Tucker that they first thought of a possible vocation when a religious whom they respected encouraged them
to consider it. Some had not thought themselves "good
enough" until a friend recognized their strengths and pointed
them out. Many of us are inclined to be leery of putting pressure on anyone where religious vocations are concerned, so
we adopt a hands-off policy. But the fact of the matter is that
many young people feel very shy about bringing the topic up
and welcome approaches from others.[6]

Some studies, particularly older ones, have shown that
priests and parents, particularly mothers, have also been in-
fluential in encouraging vocations. Unfortunately, religious
were so busy dealing with their own agendas during the years
following Vatican II that they lacked the time and energy to
share their deliberations and conclusions with bishops, priests,
and the laity. Some reacted very negatively when it seemed
to them that religious were discarding their traditions in favor
of superficialities. The tensions and disarray that were com-
municated all too often did not reassure them about the state
of religious life. It is not surprising, then, that many parents
and priests—and even religious themselves—stopped encouraging young people to consider a religious vocation and,
indeed, counseled them *not* to consider it. With these groups
as with potential recruits, religious need to share the story of
their lives and provide opportunities for them to learn about
and come to understand religious life as it is lived today.

Dolores Curran, who interviewed 128 Catholic parents who
were very active in their churches, asking if they would like
a child to enter religious life, and why or why not, gives us
some hope. Some said they would not like their children to
espouse a life "fraught with tension, unhappiness and constant soul-searching." Others, however, felt that it could be
"a satisfying, faith-filled, caring profession in a world that is
becoming increasingly secular and technological."[7]

In discussing the segments of the population from which new recruits might be expected to come, serious concern was expressed about conditions which might be encountered by immigrants, minorities, and the poor, should they enter communities which are basically middle class, Anglo, and white. In the nineteenth and early twentieth centuries German, French, Italian, Polish, and other ethnic religious communities were imported or founded to care for their compatriots. Culture clashes and gradual assimilation occurred as members of other ethnic groups entered these communities. Some who felt they were treated badly because of race or ethnicity founded new groups of their own, as when the Polish Sisters of St. Joseph of the Third Order of St. Francis broke away from the predominantly German School Sisters of St. Francis, or when the American Congregation was founded with Indian members from the Yankton Benedictines. We could expect to find some vocations among Blacks, Asians, and Hispanics, particularly the latter (whose parents are still encouraging religious vocations), but would we be willing and able to make the cultural adjustments that would enable them to feel comfortable? The international communities among us might have valuable lessons to teach here. Perhaps the flourishing communities of the twenty-first century will be founded by and for American Hispanics.

And what of candidates from among the poor? The Catholic immigrant population in America started on the bottom rungs of the economic ladder but has climbed to affluence and suburbia since 1950. Many religious communities have taken on middle-class values and status with the rest of Catholic culture. Would these scandalize and repel the poor who might otherwise be attracted by our work among them?

Some have suggested that we look to other eligible segments of the Catholic population, especially the widowed and divorced, for potential members. This would actually be a return to earlier practice. Quite a few nineteenth-century nuns, including several founders like Elizabeth Seton, had been married in their pre-convent days. The Visitandines gave a warm welcome to widows.

Whether religious will be able to project to these potential new members an image of their life which will attract them to choose it for themselves remains to be seen. Most commentators agree that the numbers in religious life in the future will be a fraction of what they were in the early sixties. However, historian John Padberg, S.J. reminds us of what happened in two other periods of Church history when there was a drastic decline in vocations. During the Reformation Luther, Calvin, and others "rejected the whole notion of religious life," and "monks and nuns left their orders in droves." Yet as "the Catholic reformation took root and spread," new orders sprang up and older ones revitalized themselves and prospered.[8]

In all lands touched by the French Revolution, Padberg points out, "many of the religious orders were officially abolished" and their members "turned out of their houses, and left to fend for themselves." Yet in the one hundred fifty years from the Revolution to Vatican II, "more new congregations were founded than in any comparable period in the history of the Church. More new congregations of women were founded in that century and a half than in the whole previous history of the Church."[9]

We should note that prior to the French Revolution most women's communities were cloistered and contemplative. Efforts by founders like Mary Ward and Angela Merici to establish sisterhoods which would serve humanity outside the cloister were thwarted by the Vatican, which held to centuries-old customs that were no longer adequate to serve the needs of the Church. It was only by establishing a noncanonical group that Vincent de Paul was able to form the Daughters of Charity to care for the needy wherever they were found. Governments which allowed communities to be founded or refounded after the Revolution usually insisted that they perform some visible service to society in addition to their prayer. The times demanded a shift of emphasis in the ministry of religious to more active modes of serving others. Not for a century would the Vatican give its approval to the communities which sprang up in response to these needs. It was only the overwhelming success and obvious fruitfulness of these apostolic groups that won from the Vatican a grudging consent to their existence.

A similar radical change in focus may be called for today. Students of American culture point out numerous changes since 1960 which have brought us to a new era. Anthropologist Gerald A. Arbuckle, S.M., feels that communities today need refounders, prophetic leaders who see the gap between the gospel and reality and point out ways to bridge it. They would call members to reconversion to the Lord and "invite us to join with them in pastoral initiatives that relate the Gospel message to a world markedly different from that known to the founding persons."[10] However, "it may be easier," he notes, "to establish new congregations than to revitalize existing ones. Congregational cultures are often vigorously opposed to change of the reformist quality needed."[11]

There are indications that history is repeating itself as far as the Vatican is concerned. Though it asked religious to study the gospel message, their founders' charisms, and the needs of the times and then make suitable adaptations, it is now abrogating its own directives. Members of congregations such as the Sisters of the Immaculate Heart of Mary and the Glenmary Sisters have had to withdraw from formal canonical status in order to pursue the work they felt the Spirit was calling them to do. Rome is refusing to approve constitutions drawn up after much prayer and study. And individuals who take up new ministries in order to alleviate the sufferings of the poor are being expelled from their communities by the Pope. It appears to many that the religious communities of the future will be noncanonical groups like that founded by Vincent de Paul when the Church's insensitivity to the call of the Spirit to serve contemporary needs and adapt to a changing culture made that necessary.

Indeed, we already have in our midst a model of the new form that a postconciliar community might take, in the Sisters for Christian Community, the fastest growing sisterhood in the Church. Its founder, Lillana Kopp, "dreamed . . . of the possibility of a wholly new structure for the consecrated life, a fresh creation without rents and patches, a fresh start that would obviate the present polarization and pain of renewal."[12] Urged by members of the hierarchy to found such a group herself, Kopp decided that "If it was to be truly and freely open to the needs of each moment of history, the charisms of the members, and the continuing direction of the Holy Spirit, then the seeking of canonical recognition should be postponed indefinitely—under present circumstances, perhaps forever."[13]

The group began in 1970 and now has around five hundred members, with an average of five new ones joining each month. Its members take vows of serving, loving, and listening, "contemporary counterparts of the traditional ones of poverty, chastity, and obedience, cleansed of patriarchal interpretations and archaic cultural accretions."[14] If Rome continues on its present course, Kopp sees communities opting for noncanonical status:

> If sisters' new constitutions continue to be rejected by well-meaning but uninspired clerics in Rome, if the enforced roundup of sisters back into archaic superior-dominated patterns of governance is actually accomplished, even against the collective best judgment of the sisters involved, if sisters and other Catholic women continue to be excluded from sharing genuine co-responsibility for the church as Christian community, then it

seems inevitable that some sisters must bolt free from canonical corrals.[15]

We have looked at the insights and concerns expressed by writers of the Quinn consultation papers regarding the future of religious life and some of their implications for religious communities. As we ponder directions and actions that could be taken, perhaps we can draw some inspiration from one who traveled this path before us.

Mary Ward was born in 1585 in penal England, where monasteries had been confiscated, priests were hunted down, and Catholics were subject to severe penalties. It was made known to her in a series of visions that God wished her to found a new kind of religious community for women, based on the spiritual and organizational model of the Jesuits. Though most of her convents were on the Continent, the animation and instruction of English Catholics was an important work of the group, one which required a great deal of ingenuity. How can the faith be kept alive when priests can only minister amid great danger and difficulty and sisterhoods have been dissolved? Through holy women trained in catechesis who can mix unobtrusively with people of all classes and instruct them.

Ward tells us how she inspired people to consider religious vocations as she traveled and worked in Yorkshire, Gloucester, Suffolk, and London: "My few labors were not altogether in vain, divers now living holily in various religious orders say that they left the world in great part through my conversation."[16] A biographer notes that the ability to turn companionship into friendship marked her throughout her life. The pictures in the *Painted Life* series done within forty years of her death give us a charming view of "the friendship enjoyed by the first companions. They sit talking together in delightful red, blue and green taffeta gowns with animation conveyed by their gesticulating hands. An insert shows them at table, enjoying being together and the support of their shared vocation."[17]

Like the Jesuits, her sisters were to be *available*, to serve the changing needs of the contemporary Church. In a vision which clarified some of her thinking about her institute, she was attracted by "justice, and those that in former times were called just persons," "works of justice," "and that we be such as we appear, and appear such as we are."[18] The "state of justice and virtue of sincerity" appeared "especially requisite as a ground of all those other virtues necessary to be exercised by those of this Institute."[19]

Ward felt the Spirit calling her and her sisters to an apostolic life in the world, something contrary to the decrees of the Council of Trent, which insisted that all religious women should be cloistered: "We feel within ourselves the pious desire—infused into us, we trust, by God—to embrace the religious state and at the same time to devote ourselves . . . to the performance of those works of Christian charity towards our neighbor that cannot be undertaken in convents."[20] She was pressured to use one of the rules that had already been approved by the Church but knew that it would never serve the revolutionary type of community she envisioned. It was to be expected that Ward's bold response to the needs of the time and the promptings of the Spirit would provoke persecution by authorities eager to uphold traditional modes of religious life. The complaints lodged against the institute in Rome deserve to be quoted at length for what they tell us about the group:

> The English ladies conform themselves to the ways of seculars. They are idle and talkative. They speak at meetings on spiritual matters, even in the presence of priests, and give exhortations, to which they are trained in their noviceship. After they have gained entrance into titled families they teach the catechism even to men, instructing them to make acts of contrition, meditation and other spiritual practices. They gad about in town and country. It sometimes happens that they are together with

men alone; they even associate with bad characters. They allow their pupils to act plays and to speak in public. They gad about in order to attract young women to enter with them. They are not solidly established financially. They cannot, like other convents, live on the interest of the members' dowries. The English Ladies despite their absence of enclosure and their unmonastic way of life, wish to be regarded as an order and give themselves out as such. They want to be religious but not monastic.[21]

Pope Urban VII suppressed the institute (which was compared to "weeds in a cornfield" which needed to be uprooted), and Mary Ward was imprisoned. But God had revealed to her that "to help to save souls is a far greater gift than the religious life or even martyrdom itself," so she was not unduly disturbed.[22] Mary Ward's sisters continued their good works as a noncanonical sisterhood. Long after her death the Vatican gave her Institute of the Blessed Virgin Mary the approval she had sought for it in 1616. In 1984 its members numbered 4,600 throughout the world.

At least one piece of research indicates that we may be heading toward the sort of "ministry of conversation" which drew so many new members into Mary Ward's institute. Research on the characteristics of women who enter religious life and remain ("persisters," they are called) shows that they reject traditional feminine roles, are active and assertive in their relationships with others, are energetic, talkative, creative, self-confident, gregarious, relaxed, psychologically healthy, honest, and sincere.[23] These are the very types that did *not* persevere in religious life in the decades prior to the council.[24]

As the writers of the Quinn consultation papers have made very clear to us, there is no secret about what it takes for religious communities to thrive: happy, holy members, supportive communities, a clear and credible mission, and the ability to convey the essence of these to others. Putting the theory into practice is the hard part. Would that all religious could have the experience of the sister who expressed her delight that such wonderful persons were choosing to enter her congregation. A young sister responded simply, ''But you're the reason we came!''

Notes

1. ''Vocation Trends: The Sisters of St. Joseph 1650–1985,'' *Quinn Consultation Paper* (hereafter *QCP*) 15.

2. ''Pyschological Aspects of the Vocation Shortage,'' *QCP*, 5.

3. Laurie Felknor (ed.) *The Crisis in Religious Vocations* (New York: Paulist Press, 1989) 36–37.

4. ''Why So Few Vocations?'' *Human Development* 7, no. 1 (Spring 1986) 21.

5. Felknor, 181–96.

6. QCP, 6.

7. ''Why Parents Don't Encourage Their Children to Be Priests and Nuns,'' *Origins* 13, no. 481 (December 29, 1983) 180.

8. Felknor, 20–21.

9. *Ibid.* 22.

10. *Ibid.* 204–6.

11. *Ibid.*

12. *Midwives of the Future,* ed. Ann Patrick Ware (Kansas City, Mo.: Leaven Press, 1985) 214.

13. *Ibid.*

14. *Ibid.* 215.

15. *Ibid.* 217.

16. Lavinia Byrne, *Mary Ward* (Dublin: Carmelite Centre of Spirituality, 1984) 12.

17. *Ibid.* 13.

18. *Ibid.* 18.

19. *Ibid.*

20. *Ibid.* 34.

21. *Ibid.* 24.

22. *Ibid.* 7.

23. P. Watson, ''Persistence Factors in Vocational Choice'' (Ph. D. diss. University of Detroit, 1955) *passim.*

24. C. Weisgerber, *Psychological Assessment of Candidates for a Religious Order* (Chicago: Loyola University Press, 1969).

These carefully prepared reflections on the future of religious life by Ritamary Bradley, S.F.C.C., professor emerita of English, St. Ambrose University, Davenport, Iowa, give insight into the value of and precedent for the noncanonical forms of religious life emerging in our time. Sister Ritamary, one of the leaders of the Sister Formation movement during the 1950s and a frequent contributor to the continuing dialogue regarding renewal, is a member of the Sisters for Christian Community, a noncanonical group of women founded in 1970, whose goal is to help remind and move the Church to the gospel truth of equality among Christians and, in particular, the equality of women.

As a perceptive interpreter of the mystics and both student of and participant in important moments in the history of religious life of women in the Church, she recognizes the complexity of the problem of identifying the essence of a constantly evolving phenomenon like that of religious life. What have become canonically recognized religious orders began as more flexible, supple, vital groups, often nearly indistinguishable from groups or individuals who did not receive formal canonical status.

Thus Sister Ritamary appeals to history to base her claim that what have been called ''essential elements'' of religious life—a regulated common life, physical proximity of the members, and a Church-approved rule—may not be such in historical fact. Sister Ritamary sets her appreciation of the gift and value of celibacy and of serious concern for a life of prayer within the context of witness and mission, within which context she likewise names the importance of proper education, suitable environment, and appropriate living and working conditions for women religious if their witness is to be complete.

5

Religious Life in the Future: Historical Precedents for Emerging Paradigms

Ritamary Bradley, S.F.C.C.

Writing on the future of religious life requires a complex methodology. One has to work out a projection from such components as the history of communities, patterns of faith experience, and the situation within communities at the present time, including the impact of a rapidly changing world. At their best, such conjectures are apt to be imprecise.

As background we ask what is the impulse which gives rise to religious life movements? Founders see an area of Christian life being neglected, in whole or in part, by the Church, especially the governing institutions of the Church. Moved by the situation and by a scriptural theme or even a text which gives direction to change, these founders step into the gap and give new witness to the presence of Christ among us. In this effort they find ties with the life of faith among other Christians; for, as Annette Walters, C.S.J., wrote in 1966: "Religious communities are especially needed to point to the goal toward which the People of God is moving. It is their function to show what is going on in a hidden way among all faithful Christians."[1]

In the light of this premise I will mention some crucial signs of change in the immediate past of religious communities; then

73

I will describe some of the trends in their present situation, and try lastly to point to some directions that may characterize the future of that multiformed tradition which we call religious life.

The Immediate Past

A distinguishing characteristic of religious life within the past forty years—since the 1950s—is the interactions among groups hitherto rigidly separated from one another. The Sister Formation Conference was a force in bringing about this interaction.[2] Responding to the call of Pius XII to religious orders to update and to prepare their members to serve on an equal basis with their lay counterparts in the professions, United States sisters in particular, working together, made deep changes in their way of life. They formulated a goal of integrating in their lives what male writers of devotional literature had portrayed as competing elements—spiritual and intellectual growth. Before Vatican Council II the sisters had already sought together for the spirit of their founders and were therefore ready and apt for the summons that followed the council: to enter into a period of experimentation for ten years. But just when the fruits of that period were becoming visible, the Vatican called a halt and ordered a return to the old ways. This command was formalized in a document called *The Essentials of Religious Life*. The National Coalition of American Nuns spoke for many others when they retitled the regressive work "The Nonessentials of Religious Life," referring to such details as habits and strict horariums. Along with this document the Vatican initiated an investigation into religious life in the United States. In the preface to a book in which nineteen American sisters told their own stories, Ann Patrick Ware, the editor, wrote:

> The idea for this book came in the midst of a discussion by sisters about the Vatican-initiated investigation of "religious life"

in the United States. Sisters rightly felt that their mode of life was likely to be scrutinized more closely than that of religious congregations of brothers or of priests. How, someone wondered, are we to let the investigating commission know what renewal of religious life in the post-Vatican II church has meant to us? Even more pointedly, did we ourselves know what renewal had meant in our lives? . . . Here, then, are the stories which answer the question that no one has ever asked American sisters. What have the vast changes during the years of experimentation in the post-Vatican church meant in your life?[3]

The shock waves in response to the Vatican's negative responses to renewal were wide and deep. They are still being felt.

The encounter was foreshadowed in part by what happened to the Sister Formation Conference in 1964. After the founding of the conference, what is now the Leadership Conference of Women Religious came into being. It was not grassroots, like SFC, but official and came under the legislative control of what is now CRIS—the Vatican bureau controlling religious orders.* The Sister Formation Conference by certain maneuvers was suppressed, and the LCWR remained in its dependent status in relation to the Vatican. LCWR has had its glorious moments, as when its president, Theresa Kane, R.S.M., spoke in the presence of papal power about the aspirations of women to equality in the Church. It has also had its episodes of shame, as when its leadership failed to press that same question in an official meeting with Vatican officials, even when the item was on the prepared agenda.[4] The incident highlights the ambivalence religious communities experience in dealing with the Vatican.

*Editor's note: When this paper was written, the Congregation for Institutes of Consecrated Life and Societies of Apostolic Life had the name Congregation for Religious and Secular Institutes (CRIS).

Coping with the Present

The current situation of religious orders of women is shadowed by a fear of loss of canonical status if there is not careful conformity to the details—often exasperating—required by CRIS. Such a situation of fear is unworthy of the gospel, which is a call to freedom. It also unjustly diverts the energies of the orders from the very purpose of witness or mission for which they exist. It poses the danger of internal dissensions, since members who have a grievance may appeal to a higher authority instead of working out difficulties within a sisterhood of equals. It offers the temptation to solidify at the local level in a game-playing strategy by which the orders will accept the wording of the legislator but reserve to themselves the interpretation which they feel safeguards their way of life.

It is not the religious orders who should be beset by fear. Rather, CRIS should fear for its failure to support and affirm the movement of the Spirit within the religious orders, for its blind adherence to legalism in the face of change, and above all for its lack of insight into what the orders have accomplished in meeting new challenges. CRIS is troubled by an obsession with controlling the lives of women and with dismay that in some places the actual number of professed religious is diminishing markedly.

In fact, it is true, of course, that some religious orders are unmistakably dying out. When this is the case, the community in question should waste no time in working out relationships with CRIS. I have observed sadly and rather close at hand the Sisters of Syon in South Brent, Devon, England, where only two sisters remain who are young and strong enough to play a part in the upkeep of the house. The others—about eight—are aged and infirm. Syon, founded in the fourteenth century according to the Briggittine rule, has had a glorious history: it is the oldest continuously existing religious house in England. Even under the expulsion of the orders in the sixteenth century, though Syon went into exile, it retained some English members. The house has been heroically faithful to its rule and to its cloistered life of contemplation. As hope for new members fades, there is nothing for Syon to do except to transmit its history and its wealth of manuscripts to safekeeping for future generations. If there were any temptation to romanticize and gloss over any less-than-ideal moments in its history, all that would be pointless now. This history is their ongoing legacy to Church and society. And that is enough and great in itself. The nuns have affiliated as ''honorary monks'' those men who are assisting in the preservation of that history. The active nuns live out, with heroic witness of trust and peace, the pain of seeing their order come to an end.

But if an order is still vigorous, out of respect for its traditions the members may want to seek an honorable accommodation with the governance of CRIS. Such is the case with the Trappists and Trappistines. They are recognizing that the future must incorporate the reality of the changing status of women. One step taken to shape their future was a joint meeting in Rome in 1987 (from mid-November to mid-December) to develop new content for their constitutions. Though it may not yet be allowed to have formally mixed chapters, mixed ''meetings'' are possible. This mixed meeting decided on the procedure of interdependent chapters: that is, men and women will meet separately and reach their decisions separately. But the men's decisions must secure approval from the women's chapter, and the women likewise must await confirmation of their decisions from the men. Thus, final decisions are mutually agreed upon. Men and women may be present at each other's chapters, while not taking part in formulating decisions. All of these changes are a conscious move toward establishing mutuality between women and men, a situation they believe existed in part in their early history.

Other communities find in their history a well-defined female independence which can now be highlighted and extended. Two movements, rooted in the Middle Ages, point the way to some of the changes reluctantly being tolerated in our times. I refer to the anchorites and the beguines. The anchorites are a witness from another time that community of dwelling is not an essential element in religious life. Though guided by a common religious tradition and legacy of rules, the anchoresses lived their lives of prayer and often of pastoral counseling in isolation from others, though they were conscious of being part of an established movement. Though there was a parallel movement among men, and men have left a legacy of rules, the anchoresses have handed on the richer tradition of contemplative teaching. There is therefore worthy precedent for the growing abandonment by many orders of the requirement of a regulated common life with physical proximity of the members.

The beguine movement, which flourished widely in the Middle Ages and did not completely die out even with Church efforts at suppression, offers another insight into tradition. These women, living alone or in houses of their own choosing, did not seek an approved rule. They focused on prayer and service to one another and the needy. Out of the movement in the twelfth and thirteenth centuries came some extraordinary women, strong in their individuality and their influence on others. Among the best known are Mechthild of Magdeburg, Hildegard of Bingen, Hadewych of Brabant, and Beatrice of Nazareth—though some of these were also connected with established orders. These beguines, and the women whom they nurtured, moved away from the ascetic rigidities required in the official orders, dimmed the distinction between lay and religious (they were, in fact, lay), and showed the path to a program of simplicity of life guided by the gospel and inspired by love. So a Church-approved rule is not an essential element of religious life. In fact, it may even be an obstacle to the underlying aims of some religious.

Such is the opinion of a recent writer, Louis Dupré, who says of the beguines:

> Part of their success they may well have owed to a relative scarcity of canonically organized religious communities of women before the Cistercians started theirs. This allowed women greater freedom in choosing their own religious structures unencumbered by constrictive traditions and uncongenial companionships.[5]

Dupré says further:

> Thus emerged those loose communities of women, derogatively called *beghines*, living without public vows, in separate little dwellings clustered around a church in a relatively open compound. These and similar spiritual sororities preceded the activity of the mendicant orders in bringing an intensive religious life to the laity through non-hierarchical channels. In northern Europe the democratization of piety and even the use of the vernacular in religious matters owes much to these impressive women.[6]

Aware of such precedents, some communities are looking into the option of forming a noncanonical branch of the canonical orders. This promising movement should be carefully studied. It could become a more or less long-lasting arrangement, accommodating the vision and experience of members of the community who wish to adhere to a tradition and yet to shed the hampering effects of an inconsistent, costly, male-dominated direction from the Vatican. Members of such a noncanonical branch would differ from associates, who are now connected with many communities. Such members would share fully in the life, traditions, and dedication of the congregation but would not submit to Vatican regulation.

My own community, the Sisters for Christian Community, founded by Lillanna Kopp in 1970 and now blessed with over five hundred members worldwide, has its roots in the traditions which built on the independence of women religious. But even more significantly, the S.F.C.C. has confronted needed change within the Church. In its simple gospel profile, containing adaptations of the traditional vows, the community takes as its goal to help move the Church from its pre-Vatican II mentality to the equality among Christians called for since we have been reminded that we are the Church. Thus, a goal is embraced corporatively, but individuals pursue that goal in diverse ways.

In dispensing themselves from the muddied formalities of canonical approval, while keeping integral ties with the Church in all its aspects, the Sisters for Christian Community are also a reminder about the place of women. The equality of women is one of those gospel truths neglected within the official Church, and hence it calls for an affirmation among religious communities. Members of S.F.C.C. generally share the common religious experience of having felt deeply in their own lives the shattering insight that the Church does not see them as complete human beings, since it still thinks of the male as the norm of human nature. Many of the members come from canonical communities where they knew firsthand the interference exerted by CRIS in the workings of communities of women.

Since some progress has been made in awareness of what women are calling for, it is easy to forget at times how entrenched the officials of the Church still are in the anti-gospel heresy that women have an inferior nature and a subordinate role willed by God.

Recent popes have reaffirmed this error. While Pius XII opened the doors to the advancement of women religious, urging them to become equals with their lay counterparts and without specifying any difference of gender, that same pontiff commanded wives to remain in a state of inequality: ''. . . he warned: 'Many voices will suggest . . . a proud autonomy; they will repeat that you are in every respect the equal of your husband, and in many respects his superior. Do not react like Eve to these lying, tempting, deceitful voices.' " [7]

Paul VI as late as 1974 gave continuity to the myth that woman has her meaning in her service to man. And even though he presents an idealized version of the female, the danger is that the basic assumption—woman is for the comfort of man—may translate in other contexts into the degradation and abuse of woman for the perceived desires of man. This female whom the Pope describes is a fantasy, at the best a projection of the undeveloped anima in the male. There is no way an authentic woman could coexist with this fantasy:

> As we see her, woman is a vision of virginal purity . . . she is for man in his loneliness the companion whose life is one of unreserved loving dedication, resourceful collaboration and help, courageous fidelity and toil, and habitual self-sacrifice. . . . She is the Mother—Let us bow in reverence before her.[8]

This fantasy, though well intentioned, is of a piece with the fantasy Geoffrey Chaucer puts in the mouth of the aging knight, January, in "The Merchant's Tale." January dreamed of finding such a vision for a wife, and believed that then he would be in paradise. His rude awakening is part of the satire of the story.

Existing communities, in many instances, are repudiating these outdated positions on women. But given their juridical subordination to the men in Rome, they may have to look forward to some hard decisions in the near future, perhaps direct confrontation with that authority if a crisis case occurs. Even the most praiseworthy ministries need to be completed by witness to the equality of women. Writing on the admirable work of the Maryknoll sisters in Nicaragua, a recent author makes that same point:

> In the Ocotal locale, Sisters Joan Uhlen and Pat Edmiston began work in the mid-1970s with weekend workshops for

women. The aim of these workshops was to enable women to recognize their own worth by drawing them out of their timidity and fear and providing a community in which they could have an expanded role as dedicated Christians. . . . While there is a new approach to women in the base communities, one finds no evidence of a frontal attack on the church's historical role in legitimizing and reinforcing male domination. A radical critique and repudiation of the basically patriarchal ideology and structure of the traditional Roman Catholic Church still needs to be addressed.[9]

It is true, of course, that communities delay freeing themselves from canonical status because they can take advantage of having the authority that governs them situated at a distance. Theoretically, a distant authority is less likely to interfere in the affairs of the community. Some sisters may even have accepted the argument made a few years ago by an official representative of CRIS when he said that the role of his congregation was to protect the women's orders from their bishops. But modern communication and air travel minimize the effect of distance, and the Vatican has interfered in recent times more radically in the internal workings of women's communities than has the episcopacy. In addition, canonical communities may trust in the security of a structured way of life, standardized by a central authority.

But in our day, in the context of movements designed in the name of religion, there is a special danger arising from such a structured way of life. That danger is the formation of cults. If communities draw new members who have a special need to be dependent on the group, if they are persons alienated from society at large, the group may acquire the characteristics of a cult. Huge amounts of corporately held property are also consistent with cult formation. This pattern has its obvious perils, not the least of which is the failure of the communities to look to solidarity with the poor. News reports on approved communities established by a breaking off from orders which are adapting and changing make this very charge against the canonically recognized new groups—that they may be near to becoming a cult.[10]

What Lies Ahead?

So what lies ahead for religious communities of women? We began with the principle that religious show visibly what is going on in a hidden way among other Christians. That is still true, though these latter are becoming more visible and articulate. It would be a mistake, however, to assume that orders can forget their role and affiliate with all who come, no matter what their lifestyle, whether married or not. The married cannot be sure of passing on to their children the ideals which they themselves wish to embrace, or even the ministries which they support. And husband and wife, even without children, may grow at different paces in their understanding of what is called for by the Christian life. There remains a work for the religious communities, not rigidly separate from their brothers and sisters, but dedicated to a lifetime witness of vowed celibacy.

As to its contemporary relevance, celibate life for women overall is a move toward equality with men. Such a life shows that women have meaning in their own persons, not just with reference to the male. And celibate women should repudiate the claim that their meaning derives from taking on spiritual motherhood instead of physical motherhood. Nuns are not mothers at all: they are friends of others in Christ. They are sisters in the broad sense, adult sisters, on a par with adult brothers and friends. The true mother, as Julian of Norwich has so compellingly taught, is Christ. She goes so far as to say that the very motive of Christ's becoming flesh was to become our mother in all things, whereas, as the Word, that motherhood lacked the dimension of humanity.

But society has its doubts about religious life as it is taking shape today, doubts arising in part from entrenchment in the old images and ideas. First, some will ask: But what is the difference between nuns today—with their individuality of dress and their freedom of action—and other single women, for example, those in the professions? Let it be stressed that there does not have to be much difference (nuns are not vowed to being different); but there often is. Single women not vowed to celibacy at times seem ambivalent about their position in society, which still looks askance on those who do not marry. Such women may put their total lives together differently than nuns, choosing other priorities, measuring success by other norms. Sometimes they wonder if they have "missed something" and show embarrassment when the conversation of married people centers on their children. Nuns have the advantage of the long tradition which enhances their way of life, flawed though the rationale for that tradition often is. Fundamentally, they have chosen a way of life in view of God's love. Celibacy, which must be freely chosen, facilitates for some the "centering on one thing," the focusing of one's life in God.

Celibacy has been blamed for the shortcomings which give rise to the unflattering stereotypes of nuns as narrow, frustrated, rigid, and "sexually starved." Underlying this stereotype is the myth that a woman only becomes a woman through a male. This myth is at work in the sexual harassment of women, whether as students, divorced persons, or professionals. The message is not that women are seductive, but that they should not try to be the equals of men.

It was not celibacy but lack of adequate education, suitable environment, and appropriate formation that produced some sisters who conformed to the stereotype of being "nunny." When nuns are properly educated and provided with living and working conditions consistent with their profession or service, they behave quite differently. Such is the point of a "Hers" columnist in the *New York Times*. In fact, the message of these nun-teachers was liberation:

> The nuns were, with the exception of my family and one or two fast friends, the most important force in my formative years. It is popular now to think of them as a joke or an anachronism, to suggest that the nuns taught little more than that a well-placed ruler hurt like the dickens and that boys were only after one thing.[11]

But that, she says, was not what she learned from them at all. She learned, rather, that

> women are smart and capable, could live in community without men, and in fact did not need men much . . . I suspect, deep down, that some of these women turned me into a feminist . . . I never heard a word about sex from the nuns. . . . Above all, it seemed to me that the nuns who taught us had their own lives much more so than my mother, who was parceled out to many others, our family's community property.[12]

The ministries which religious engage in make more sense to skeptics about religious life than any other component. These may also be shared with others who are not in communities. But most importantly, a serious concern for a life of prayer is an unbreakable link between religious and others, without denying the lifestyle of either. It does not require strict community of life nor commonality of service and mission. Nor does it require a regimented prayer schedule approved by male authorities who may or may not experience such a life themselves.

These observations are perhaps too obvious to share with those who are already in religious communities and committed to such a way of life. But they stand on the position that the varied history of religious life has still many forms to unfold. These forms are responses to a certain intransigence within parts of the Church, to the needs of changing times, and to the ongoing calls to unconditional love for which religious life is a fitting response.

Notes

1. Annette Walters, *Religious in the Constitution on the Church* (Glen Rock, N.J.: Paulist Press, 1966) 19.

2. Mary L. Schneider, "American Sisters and the Roots of Change: The 1950s." *U.S. Catholic Historian* 7 (Winter 1988), 55–72; also Mary L. Schneider, *The Transformation of American Women Religious. The Sister Formation Conference as a Catalyst for Change* (University of Notre Dame: Cushwa Center Papers, 1986).

3. *Midwives of the Future. American Sisters Tell Their Story* (Kansas City, Mo.: Sheed and Ward, 1985) vii.

4. See LCWR's overview of its own history in *1986 Conference Report: Uncovering the Holy. Power and Meaning in Women's Experience.* (Silver Springs, Md.: LCWR). The board of the National Coalition of American Nuns published a critique of that report in its newsletter, *NCAN* 17, no. 2 (Winter 1987).

5. Louis Dupré, "General Introduction," *Light from Light. An Anthology of Christian Mysticism* (New York: Paulist Press, 1988) 20.

6. *Ibid.* But Dupré adds: "Many had to pay a high price for their independence. Some were imprisoned and several beguines died at the stake. . . . Despite repression and the prerogative of a male clergy to teach and to test theological doctrine, spiritual women in subsequent centuries continued to impose their spiritual authorities upon their contemporaries."

7. "To all Italian Women," October 1945, 131; and "To All Newly Weds," September 1941, 68–69, in *The Woman in the Modern World: Papal Teachings.* Benedictine Monks of Solesmes (Boston: St. Paul Editions, 1959). Cited in *Women, Religion and Social Change*, eds. Yvonne Haddad and Ellison Banks Findly (Albany: State University of New York Press, 1985) 459.

8. "The Rise of Women in Contemporary Society," Address of Pope Paul VI to the Convention of the Union of Italian Catholic Jurists, in *The Pope Speaks*, December 8, 1974 (Spring 1975). Cited in *Women, Religion and Social Change*, 459.

9. *Women, Religion and Social Change*, 339–440.

10. See, for example, the newspaper publicity dealing with the canonical communities of Shaw Island.

11. Anna Quindlen, "Hers," *New York Times* (March 20, 1986) 22.

12. *Ibid.*

In looking to the future, Joseph Schmidt, F.S.C., currently serving in Romeoville, Illinois, as secretary of formation for the Brothers of the Christian Schools of the United States and Canada, analyzes four areas of religious life in which changes are taking place today and tries to discern what new forms may evolve. Noteworthy is his emphasis upon the need for "mystics" (Rahner's term for persons contemplatively aware) and his suggestion that future canon law may need to allow for changed membership patterns. Brother Joseph observes that leadership for change will come not through official strategies but through persons who have experienced needs of ministry, of prayer life, and of community and have begun to live in ways that respond to those needs. In his paper Brother Joseph also takes account of statistics regarding women and men and reflects on the implications of such data for the future (cf. the findings of Marie Augusta Neal, S.N.D. de Namur, in, for example, Catholic Sisters in Transition: From the 1960s to the 1980s, Wilmington: Glazier, 1984; and the interview with Donna Markham, O.P., in New Catholic World, January–February 1988).

6

The Future of Religious Life

Joseph Schmidt, F.S.C.

While it is impossible to know the specific details of what the future of religious life might include, I believe it is accurate to say that, given our historical period over the next fifty years, (1) some current religious communities will not survive; (2) some religious communities will continue, but with some change; and (3) new religious communities will evolve. Each of these three options seems to have been the way religious life has responded to crises in the past and, I believe, can be expected to respond in the present situation.

I would like to focus on the second of these options and explore in general what changes may occur in the religious life of active communities in four specific and interrelated areas. These four areas are community, prayer, ministry, and membership. I will then conclude with a final reflection on how we might be led into the future.

Community

The cultural phenomenon of individualism, loneliness, and alienation has made community life all the more attractive in our time. Some studies have indicated that one of the major reasons, at least among men, for being attracted to religious life is the appeal of community living and sharing which offers opportunities for mutual personal support as well as team ministry. It is ironic that, at the very time when those outside religious life are attracted to the role community plays in religious life, those in religious life, especially in middle years, are finding that it is precisely the lack of community which is most distressing. One of the most common reasons given for withdrawing from religious life today is the lack of a sense of community support and the dearth of personal sharing.

Community, in the sense of gospel love lived out (and not, of course, of unhealthy dependency), is a gift which religious give not only to one another and not only to those in their ministry but also to the world. Community life is proof that gospel love is possible. I believe it is even proper to say that the very essence of religious life is lived gospel love, and the very essence of the religious apostolate is proclaiming its possibility.

I see three elements in the form that community may take in the future. The first is a more conscious commitment to a sustained and regular "presence with" other members of the group, including especially times of sharing faith, prayer, and worship, and possibly sharing ministry. A second element is a more conscious commitment to a "presence for" other members of the community, including a personal ministry to other members of the group in times of particular need. Finally, I see community being expressed in a "presence to" others in the form of hospitality and in accompanying those others.

Whereas community in the past has often meant physical proximity and uniformity, community as it presently is emerging will put more emphasis on quality of time involved in "presence with," "presence for," and "presence to." This will have implications in terms of practical living situations, the use of personal time, individual and community lifestyle, the use of authority, and the notion of mutuality. In addition, some religious communities in the future will almost certainly combine women and men celibates in community living and will probably include some membership arrangement for married couples.

Prayer

Rahner has remarked that in the future the religious person will be a mystic or not religious at all. I would take this to mean that, as a life based on faith becomes more and more countercultural in the face of consumerism and a pleasure/power orientation, the person living the life of faith will do so not from any support of the culture but from inner conviction that comes from experience. This seems to have already begun to happen with the upheaval caused by Vatican II.

Teresa of Avila mentions that the devil intimidates those who know of God's mercy only by faith and not by experience. I take Teresa's comment to be supplementary to Rahner's. Teresa seems to be suggesting that even the discipline, practice, ideology, and teaching of the institutional Church or of a religious community is not capable of sustaining the life of faith of the individual; the only real validity for a life of faith comes from the personal experience of "knowing" God's mercy in our life story.

It is a phenomenon of today's society that many persons caught in the rush of activities—often activities of acquisition, pleasure, power, and production—have little time or inclination to reflect on or understand what they are experiencing in their life story. Awareness has been diminished in our society and replaced with compulsion.

While I do not presume to identify the particular forms that prayer might take in religious life, it is, perhaps, safe to suggest that a deeper contemplative spirit, a spirit of attention to the realities of life in which the presence of God is found, will have increasing importance. A conscious and committed relationship to Christ will be more solidly experienced and appropriately expressed. This will, of course, have specific implications regarding the use of personal and communal time and resources in a lifestyle that makes prayer a priority.

While it is true in a sense to say that all of our ministry is a sharing of community, it seems that we can say with even more truth that all of our ministry is a sharing of the spirit of faith and spirit of prayer.

Ministry

It seems to be a historical fact that most religious communities, especially those established in the nineteenth century from which most present-day active communities have their roots, were founded in response to the needs of the poor and those who needed a particular service. Many of these groups originally developed in an almost spontaneous way and were subsequently subsumed canonically as religious communities. Once subsumed, they were incorporated into categories with specific responsibility relative to the larger institutional Church.

Our own day has seen an upsurge in societal organizations assuming many of the charitable works which had previously been done by religious. In fact, a particular problem in religious communities today is that some members find it difficult to involve themselves in works which are a challenge to and expression of their sense of faith caring. This because either the institute must charge for services and therefore cannot extend them to the truly needy, or because there is a professionalism required in services which many older members of religious communities do not have. Presently, some services to those who are truly needy—services which would be in conformity with the intent of the original foundation—must at times be done on a more voluntary and, therefore, more limited basis: ministry to the sick, prison ministry, education of the very poor.

There is some statistical evidence, especially regarding women considering entering religious life, that the kind of ministry in which the community is involved is an important motivating force. One of the prime general categories to which potential religious life candidates are attracted in ministry is working with the poor, the outcasts of society, the oppressed, and the truly neglected.

While, again, it is impossible to determine the particulars, it can be suggested that the ministry of religious communities of the future will be more committed, in personnel and resources, to one or both of the following forms of apostolate: direct service to the poor and needy who are neglected or to the outcasts of society, or advocacy on their behalf. In our present society either of these kinds of ministry, or a combination of both, would inevitably lead to a confrontation with society over values, goals, and the use of resources. In particular, such ministry would have implications in the areas of power, justice, use of the environment, and peace.

Membership

Traditionally, religious communities have had a clear definition of membership. This definition has almost always been dictated by canon law and has invariably included permanency and celibacy. This arrangement has had very laudable effects. Many cultural changes, however, make it seem clear that membership in religious orders in the future might well take forms which would include various levels of permanency and commitment and not be reserved exclusively for celibates. (Celibacy has always been a canonical condition for religious life; and so by suggesting that religious life could include noncelibate members, the canonical definition of religious life is being extended.)

It is quite possible that future religious communities may consist of core members whose commitment would be permanent and would be expressed particularly in celibacy. At the same time, these religious groups might also include members with a temporary commitment, proclaimed from the beginning as such, members who may or may not make a temporary celibate commitment. Finally, religious groups might also include married couples (and by extension, children) in either a permanent or temporary arrangement. This form of community life would witness to both the uniqueness and complementarity of Christian celibacy and marriage in the Church. The binding force of the religious community would be the common allegiance to the religious spirit celebrated and proclaimed by the group as well as to the apostolic ministry to which the group was dedicated. While not attempting to focus on the particulars, I think it is clear that religious groups with varied membership would modify their lifestyle considerably from that of present-day religious communities. It is also obvious that vocation and formation work in such communities would take on new forms.

Presently there are groups in the larger Church which have this varied kind of membership. These are not canonical religious communities, but they are committed Church groups and may offer the kind of model for a form of future religious life. They include Agape Community, Sojourners Community, and Catholic Worker.

Movement into the Future

While there are many ways of envisioning how religious communities will adapt and move into the future, I would like to focus on one in particular. Many strategies for change suggest the use of brainstorming, statistics, and cultural analysis. While respecting these methods, I would like to emphasize the organic continuity of change which evolves through the awareness of the group, and in particular through the awareness of individuals.

Historically, religious renewal has often occurred through the emergence of one or two individuals within the community who have assumed a leadership role, even if unconsciously. Vatican II has been an important instrument in raising the awareness of religious regarding adaptation as well as providing the institutional approval for renewal, but the actual renewal itself will probably come from leadership provided by one or two individuals in a given religious community.

The leadership of change has often not been provided by official strategies but rather by those who have begun to live in ways which have responded to the personally experienced needs of the apostolate, of prayer life, and of community life. In other words, the renewal has emerged more often from a response of the "heart" than from a calculation of the "head."

In this sense, renewal can be endorsed by superiors, encouraged by committees, approved by chapters, and legitimatized by councils; but the form that it takes will begin to emerge through the activities of one or several members as they live out their own vision and the understanding of their call within the religious group.

To be open and responsive to individuals who, perhaps, cannot be designated beforehand as being such leaders is an important role of official community leadership. This, of course, presents a significant challenge to official leadership because it calls them to take the initiative in identifying and encouraging change. At the same time it asks them to open themselves to individuals within the community who are inaugurating change through their own personal initiatives in ways which are not necessarily officially predetermined.

Part III
The Contemplative Call

Although Vatican II, with its renewed ecclesiology, tried to place both the Mother of God and contemplative nuns within their rightful context as part of the people of God, other postconciliar forces, operating out of outworn symbols, have resisted this ecclesiology and have blocked the efforts of nuns who have accepted it. This is one of the points made by M. Clare Adams, O.S.C., a member of the Poor Clare community in Minneapolis, Minnesota, and a graduate of Yale Divinity School and the School of Philosophy at The Catholic University of America. Her paper offers a thorough account of a largely unpublicized story of nuns since Vatican II. In telling this story Sister Clare reflects on the symbols and myths that have undergirded the structure of canonical contemplative life and the purposes which she finds such myths and symbols serve: a notion of holiness that rejects the body and a feminism that desires to keep women out of reach and out of sight. Sister Clare traces in detail the history and power of these myths and symbols as they have shaped the actual treatment of nuns. She reflects on their inappropriateness today and in the future, as nuns meet with resistance on the part of Church authorities when they try to live according to new symbols coming out of a Vatican II ecclesiology. She notes that under the guise of protection, nuns have been discriminated against; this "can in no way provide the design for a Church of the future." Toward the end of her paper Sister Clare outlines eight phases in the process of renewal that could serve as a paradigm for other persons or groups struggling to implement the new understandings of Vatican II in a Church wounded by sin.

7

Nuns Since Vatican II: Symbol, Myth, and Reality

M. Clare Adams, O.S.C.

Preface

In March of 1985 the Leadership Conference of Women Religious (LCWR) presented a statement to the ad hoc committee of bishops who were holding hearings on the proposed pastoral on women. In this statement, prepared by the national board, the LCWR identified "structural change which addresses alienating factors" as one of the "conditions which contribute to the reconciliation of women." The statement stressed the importance of "the structures of language, symbol, image . . ." not only as revealing "our world views, values and attitudes . . ." but as a "potent formative agent," and noted that the "liberation of human beings is closely related to the liberation of "such linguistic/epistemological structures."[1]

In April 1988 the NCCB released the first draft of the proposed pastoral, now called a "pastoral response to women's concerns" and entitled "Partners in the Mystery of Redemption."

Among symbols needing renewal, a specific group are those surrounding the institution of nuns, "the canonical, contemplative life" or, more precisely, nuns as *cloistered* women.

This paper is a reflection on this symbol: its importance,

99

its alienating use, and its desired transformation. It represents the experience of the author and of many nuns in contemplative communities. It is not intended to deny the possibility of other experiences but to promote healthy dialogue, a dialogue already taking place, as the present draft of the pastoral records.

Introduction

The institution of nuns is an ancient symbol. In practice it replaces the earlier institution of consecrated virgins so prominent in the early Roman Church during the age of the martyrs. In its present form it also stands as an integral part of the monastic institution. With such a heritage, the institution of nuns has become and remains one of the most powerful symbols in the religious life of the West. Similarly, the myths that encompass this institution have functioned in a powerful way in fostering and maintaining certain theological perspectives and attitudes and in sustaining types of spirituality that were both familiar and deeply rooted in the world and the Church prior to Vatican II.

It would not be too much to say that the institution of nuns and the theology of contemplation, a contemplation held up to all the faithful as the ideal spiritual goal and highest form of Christian life, were two pillars that helped to support an entire edifice of spirituality and, in addition, formed the basis of a critique of other developments in the Christian community.

Not only the spiritual life of the individual member of the Church but even the kinds of religious communities were measured and valued by their approximation to the contemplative ideal—an ideal identified with, expressed in, and supported by the institution of nuns and the canonical forms in which it was preserved and codified, particularly its most essential structure, namely, enclosure. Evidence for this fact is to be found in the 1918 Code of Canon Law itself, which provided for ease of transfer from an apostolic to a contemplative community as from a "lower" to a "higher" form of life. Transfer "downward" from a contemplative to an apostolic community was not so regarded and provided for.

The perdurance of certain philosophical world views, particularly those of a Neoplatonic strain common in Christianity from early centuries, is reflected in the way enclosure of nuns is perceived. This view is embodied in the sustained canonical tradition regarding enclosure for nuns, which reached a high-water mark of codification in the eleventh and twelfth centuries and remained largely unaltered up to Vatican II. In such a vision of the world, access to the divine is achieved by separation from the world, the body, and ultimately from matter. Thus, a way of life defined by enclosure offers an ideal path and stands as a paradigm for the human search for communion with God.

The reorientation of spirituality that was characteristic of Vatican II was meant to effect a reorientation and renewal of the institution of nuns as well. This is stated in principle in *Perfectae Caritatis*, article 16, which says that "The papal cloister for nuns totally dedicated to contemplation is to be retained. Still, it should be modified according to the conditions of time and place, and outdated customs done away with."[2] In essence this reorientation derives from a profound development in the understanding of the very nature of the Church, which had come to fruition in the new ecclesiology of Vatican II; was reflected in the constitution on the Church, *Lumen Gentium*; and was understood and expressed more fully in the light of *Gaudium et Spes*.

The strength of resistance to change, however, and in particular the resistance to any change in the symbolic form of the institution of nuns, embodied primarily in the form of enclosure, made itself evident almost immediately after the council in the Norms for Implementation of *Perfectae Caritatis*

(*Ecclesiae Sanctae*) of Paul VI, dated August 6, 1966, and particularly in the later document concerning the enclosure of nuns entitled *Venite Seorsum*, promulgated by Paul VI August 15, 1969.

In the apostolic letter *Ecclesiae Sanctae* and in all the directions, letters, and instructions that have followed, a principle of exclusion has been used to withdraw nuns of canonical institutes from the ordinary structures of renewal. In effect, this has deprived them of any title in law to necessary experimentation, to internal and communal review and healthy critique of their way of life through international chapters, and to that consequent renewal of life formally promoted and required by the entire experience and mandate of the council. How is this compatible with *Lumen Gentium?* Where is that inclusion in theory and practice which led the bishops to treat the role even of the Mother of God in relation to, and not apart from, the rest of the faithful?

Underlying this history, which has followed a consistent pattern for over twenty years, are forces which are at the heart of the struggle for renewal in the Church. This pattern calls into question the honesty and obedience of Church officials themselves to the authority of an ecumenical council, and their procedures touch on the deepest assumptions and biases in the Church regarding the place of women in the schema of redemption. Just as profoundly, this struggle signals a new frontier: the challenge of recognizing and owning the experience of so many — nuns and other men and women — which involves a call to taste and share in the mystery of Christ, an experience which has been called ''contemplative'' by those who went before us. The Spirit is ever the same, but the wine is new and the old skins will not hold it.

It is because these matters apply in principle not only to nuns but to women throughout the Church, because they apply as well to the whole Church in regard to the internal relationships of members of the body of Christ one to another, and because finally they constitute part of the signs of the times to which we are called to attend that I bring forward this experience in four parts:

Part I: Historical Dimensions of the Institution of Nuns

Part II: A Summary of the Directives of Vatican II to Nuns and an Analysis of the Restrictions Placed on Nuns with Respect to These Directives by Church Authority in the Years Since Vatican II

Part III: An Analysis of the Experience of Nuns in the Form of a Paradigm of Renewal

Part IV: Summary Conclusion and Reflections

Part I: Historical Dimensions of the Institution of Nuns

The genealogy of the institution of nuns includes the order of consecrated virgins and that of monasticism. Both contribute richly to its symbolism.

The rites of solemn profession which were reserved to nuns or to those communities which by tradition professed solemn vows witness to and have their origin in the order of consecrated virgins. They differ markedly from the rituals used for religious profession of simple vows. Unlike the rites of simple perpetual profession of so many congregations of women religious, rites which frequently took place in a devotional context or, if during the Mass, had the character of an adjunct rite (after Communion, after the homily, or even at the end of the Mass), the rites of solemn profession required a clear insertion into the Eucharistic liturgy and employed a ritual that was almost identical in form with the ordination rite of deacons, with the exception of the laying on of hands.

Since Vatican II and the revision of rituals, a clearer connection has been established for all religious between the rite of religious profession and the Eucharistic liturgy, with the profession placed at the end of the Liturgy of the Word, but the revised forms clearly lack the symbolism and tradition that were formerly required for the solemn profession. Another restoration of ritual is that for the consecration of virgins. It is noteworthy that this has been reinstated as a public and canonical form of life only after the council, and only after the decision was made to eliminate the distinctions between solemn and simple vows in the new Code of Canon Law.

The historical intertwining of rituals gave great power to the profession of solemn vows for nuns. There was a combination of the vigor and ecclesial dimension of consecration, a setting apart for special ministry that was akin to the ordination of a deacon, and the ideal character of the order of virgins was revealed as a gift of the Spirit, especially in the age of the martyrs. The notion of setting apart in a physical sense as an intrinsic aspect of consecration derived neither from the vocation of the deacon nor from that of the virgin in the early Church, since enclosure, or physical separation from the world, was characteristic of neither. Rather, the notion of enclosure and setting apart in that sense grew out of a development in the monastic tradition.

Monasticism, though not as ancient as the order of deacons and of consecrated virgins, is one of the oldest institutions in the Church. As an institution it includes both monks and nuns. From a historical point of view, male and female communities developed along parallel lines with respect to lifestyle and authority, with female communities enjoying much the same autonomy as their male counterparts. There were also interesting developments such as double communities under one superior, who at times was even an abbess. Their essential difference lay only in the fact that while monks could enjoy a rather self-contained sacramental ministry once members were ordained and once the abbot came to be endowed with powers of orders and jurisdiction, female communities required the ministry of male priests to provide for their sacramental needs. This need dictated and limited their choices as to geographical location and reflected a dependence which was later extended to other aspects of their lives, but which in the early centuries in no way affected their self-determination.[3]

As the Roman Church gradually centralized, however, distinct canonical structures for female communities began to take shape with respect to authority and jurisdiction. At a high point of this process of centralization stands the constitution *Periculoso* by Pope Boniface VIII, which was issued in 1298 and which deals with preserving the integrity of the enclosure. Canonical provisions and norms articulated in this document as general law peculiar to the institution of nuns endured up to the codification of canon law in 1917, and their outlines are preserved in the revision of that code following Vatican II. The limitations surrounding enclosure gradually limited the autonomy of monasteries and their self-directing character as vested in their chapters and internal superiors. Enclosed communities of nuns gradually became highly controlled units governed from without by specific and uniform general laws under the supervision and authority of rather elaborate systems involving the bishop, cardinal protectors, and papal representatives.[4]

Article 9 of *Perfectae Caritatis* illustrates just how far this evolution has gone and how deeply it has affected perception when, after affirming the "venerable institution of monastic life," it goes on to say in the third sentence: "The main task of *monks* is to render to the Divine Majesty a service at once simple and noble, within the monastic confines" (italics mine). Although the institution of monastic life is the subject of the article, only monks are named. There is no reference to nuns, even though some orders, thoroughly monastic in origin such as Benedictines and Cistercians, include both male and female communities.

So strong is the link between "nun" and "cloister" that the "monastic woman" and the tradition to which she belongs tend to disappear. This illustrates clearly the conceptual reality fostered and expressed by the canonical reality. The male religious dedicated as a monk is seen as belonging to an institution of monasticism which article 9 goes on to extol with all its breadth, its variations, its many-leveled contributions, and its continual relation to the spiritual life of the Christian community; but in all of this passage there is no mention of nuns.[5] The woman dedicated to the same vocation has her identity only in the "canonical contemplative life." She is a *cloistered* nun. As a nun, her way of life is referred to in article 16 of the same document in relation to cloister (and implicitly in article 7, which speaks of the way of life called contemplative).

These texts reflect the historical distinction that has developed between the notion of contemplative life and monastic life. The latter tends to be seen in relation to monks and possesses its own canonical structures and a wide range of expressions. The former tends to be identified with enclosure and associated with the vocation of nuns. In a certain sense, the complete identification of the vocation of nuns with the enclosure is typified in the reform of St. Teresa of Avila. The discalced Carmelite stands as a paradigm of the institution of nuns as it has come down to us and as the embodiment or perfect symbol of its ideal.

Part II: Analytic Summary of the Status of Nuns Since Vatican II

Lumen Gentium

At the heart of the ecclesiology of *Lumen Gentium* is a clarification of the relationship of members of the Church to one another in the body of Christ. Chapter I attempts to uncover the true nature of the Church by mining the riches of biblical images such as the kingdom of God, the seed, the sheepfold, the living temple, and the body of Christ, while Chapter II develops the notion of the people of God. And it is within this vision of the Church that the constitution goes on to delineate the various vocations of its members. With respect to these diverse vocations, there is one profound principle of valuation: the call and work of the Holy Spirit. Prototypical of this vision of the Church is the way in which the role of the Mother of God is presented. Her place in the mystery of Christ is not treated in a separate document but within the context of the mystery of the Church.[6]

This perspective contrasts sharply with that which prevailed prior to the council. Before *Lumen Gentium* persons and vocations were understood largely by means of Neoplatonic categories within a hierarchical and objective world view. In such a framework, the principle of valuation was that of immateriality. Thus, whatever was more disembodied or separated from the material was considered more spiritual and closer to the divine. Persons were defined in terms of the characteristic activity that determined their state of life, and these states of life or vocations were evaluated objectively in terms of their proper rung on the hierarchical ladder.

The consequence of this was that the "more spiritual" the activity associated with a state of life, the more spiritual was the vocation considered and, by implication, the persons given to such activities. The more mundane the activity, the more involved with the material world, the "lower" or more mediated were such activities seen to be, and therefore the state of life defined by such an activity was also considered "lower." In such an economy, the "higher" vocations were seen as justified in themselves, the "lower" seen as mediated or valued as means to an end. Although it was always formally affirmed that the same holiness was accessible to all no matter what the objective (higher or lower) state of life or status of the individual vocation, an aura surrounded those states of life and persons seen to be involved in more spiritual activities.

The reality of this pervasive norm of valuation is evident in the preaching and writing on the spiritual life of this long period. Over and over it is affirmed that holiness and union with God, and even the grace of contemplation, are accessible no matter what one's state of life may be objectively. Were it not true that some states of life were perceived to be higher, some lower, and were not the principle of immateriality so dominant, spiritual guides would not have been at such pains to encourage those in the "lesser states" not to limit their spiritual hopes.

The procedures of canon law also reflected this principle. For example, by mutual consent, married persons could move to the religious life and take religious vows. An "active" religious could transfer to a "higher" institute, that is, to a contemplative institute. The single life of the layperson always stood at the bottom of the ladder and was notoriously difficult to define by these objective categories. It tended to be seen as an accident of various circumstances. Since "higher" was better, a vocational transfer in the "higher" direction could be discerned as an authentic call of the Spirit. A movement in the other, "lower" direction, while it could be provided for by dispensation, was not so regarded. Separation of married couples, for example, with a movement to the single life, was a failure of a commitment, with all of the resulting emotional consequences.

What I wish to point out here is not the various complexities or pastoral issues involved but simply the pervasiveness of the principle of valuation, in order to emphasize how radical is the shift in theological perspective represented by *Lumen Gentium*. Only very gradually is the new mentality taking root, and only slowly can it perhaps be recognized that the massive vocational transfers that have occurred since the council are part of a revision in the common vision of the mystery of the Church. We are still far from absorbing this vision emotionally at the levels of sensibility and of symbol, of claiming the peculiar Christian sense of vocation as a nonpredetermined and free gift of the Holy Spirit for the building up of the body of Christ in love.

From what has been said, therefore, it is clear that in the context of *Lumen Gentium* nuns do not stand apart from, but with, the other members of the Church. They are meant to be included in theory and in practical matters in the general teaching and directives of the council. In addition, the council indicates multiple ways in which nuns are called to share in the work of renewal. The contributions it expects of nuns touch on all the important aspects of the council as expressed in its documents. Examples are the following:

1. *Decree on Religious Life*, Perfectae Caritatis

A call to renewal and indication of the manner and the means are given in

- Article 2, which calls for a simultaneous process of return to "the original inspiration behind a given community" and for "an adjustment of the community to the changed conditions of the times." This echoes principles outlined in the apostolic constituion of Pope Pius XII in 1950 entitled *Sponsa Christi*, which will be discussed below.
- Article 16, which states that "The papal cloister for nuns totally dedicated to contemplation is to be retained. Still it should be modified according to the conditions of time and place, and outdated customs done away with. In such matters, consideration should be given to the wishes of the monasteries themselves."

2. *Decree on Ecumenism,* Unitatis Redintegratio

- Article 15, which states that "it is of supreme importance to understand, venerate, preserve and foster the . . . rich liturgical and spiritual heritage of the Eastern Churches in order to . . . bring about reconciliation between Eastern and Western Christians." And it points out that the "riches of those spiritual traditions" are those "to which monasticism gives special expression."

3. *Decree on Missionary Activity of the Church,* Ad Gentes

- Article 18, which affirms the affinity of contemplative communities for adaptation and inculturation in keeping with the spiritual traditions of other, non-Christian cultures as well as the role of these communities in evangelization: "Let them reflect attentively on how Christian religious life may be able to assimilate the ascetic and contemplative tradition whose seeds were sometimes already planted by God in ancient cultures prior to the preaching of the Gospel. . . . Worthy of special mention are the various projects aimed at helping the contemplative life take root."[7]
- Article 40, which urges contemplative communities "to found houses in mission areas. . . . Thus living out their lives in a manner accommodated to the truly religious traditions of the people, they can bear splendid witness there among non-Christians to the majesty and love of God. . . ."

4. *Declaration on the Relationship of the Church to Non-Christian Religions*

The kind of respect and inner communion with the spiritual traditions of other cultures inculcated by this declaration is heard by those in contemplative communities in a personal way. By nature, their way of life is suited to adaptation to local traditions and to a spiritual kinship with other religions. This can often be understood by non-Christians, as much experience indicates.

References such as these indicate the direct call that the council has given to nuns as well as the importance of their response to this call. This teaching of the council is broad and open ended and serves both as a guide and a motivating force.

Sponsa Christi

Earlier, in 1950, in his apostolic constitution *Sponsa Christi,* Pope Pius XII put forth a program of renewal for nuns. This document is significant for its identification of the sources of renewal, for its authorization of change in the observance of enclosure as a means to renewal, and because it implicitly contained seeds of conflict.

Sponsa Christi called for renewal and development in four areas:

1. *Work*

The Pope noted that a serious occupation was necessary for good mental health, that work was one of the ancient pillars of monastic life *(ora et labora),* and that justice required honest effort not only to support oneself and the religious community but also to provide the means to give help to those in need. He directed nuns to undertake new means of support in keeping with the times and their own talents.

2. *Education and Formation*

He stated that an education and formation for contemplative life in keeping with the natural gifts and degree of culture of each one was essential.

3. *Federation*

He strongly affirmed the value and appropriateness of cooperation and mutual assistance among monasteries and called for the establishment of federations in order to offset the isolation created by a too-strict observance of enclosure.

4. *Fostering of Charisms*

He emphasized the great variety of charisms that exist among the generic class of "canonical contemplative communities," stating that each institute had its own proper spirit and characteristic means of nurturing contemplation. He noted that the uniform type of observances that had been imposed upon all nuns had overshadowed the specific charism of each group and diminished its fruitfulness. And he called for a renewed dedication to the primacy of prayer according to the spirituality proper to each tradition.

Vatican II simply enhanced and gave full scope to all these principles.

Pope Pius XII saw that such a renewal called for an adjustment in the norms regarding cloister. He introduced a new, practical principle for defining cloister for nuns and provided for the modification of law. This found development in a document of the same year, *Inter Praeclara,* an instruction of the Congregation for Religious.

The principle introduced by Pope Pius XII concerned the relationship of the community to the apostolate. It distinguished communities wholly given to contemplation from those which combined some form of apostolic work with the canonical contemplative life. This distinction was to be reflected in two categories of papal cloister: major and minor. Major papal cloister was to be observed by communities wholly given to contemplation, minor papal cloister by those with some form of apostolate, such as the Visitation nuns who conducted convent schools. Communities such as the latter were required to make a decision: either continue such work and opt for minor papal cloister, or give up the work and adopt major papal cloister.

The purpose of the distinction was purely functional. There was no suggestion that a community "ought" to adopt a path different from the one it had traditionally taken, but it did result in each community's having to define itself according to this criterion. Other principles were included, such as that calling for the reintroduction of solemn vows where this tradition had been interrupted; and important new structures were set up, such as the possibility of federations. But it was the distinction between kinds of papal cloister that caused shock waves throughout the cloistered world.

Communities and individuals were thrust into a decision-making process about their preferred canonical identity on the basis of cloister long before they had even begun to understand, integrate, and implement the consequential theological principles regarding renewal of life given in part I of the constitution. An almost ideological line of demarcation was drawn for both individuals and communities. Orders such as the Visitation were shaken by the need to decide whether they would or would not retain their traditional schools. The result was a regrouping of personnel, with some houses opting for the life totally given to contemplation. The transfer of nuns undermined some formerly well-balanced communities, with the result that many houses were closed.

Several factors contributed to this situation. (1) The new principle of cloister set up a strict disjunction, an "either/or" framework. (2) Such a framework disallowed a certain open-mindedness and flexibility and tended to interfere with a more natural historical development. (3) Given the mentality that prevailed before the council, the terms "major" and "minor" reinforced or evoked the sense of "higher" and "lower" or "more holy" and "less holy" with respect to the two kinds of cloister. This reinforced the existing sense that the purely contemplative monastery represented a state of life somewhat superior to that which combined some apostolate with its contemplative lifestyle. This kind of evaluation reflected more a mentality common in the Church at the time than it did a mature reading of *Sponsa Christi*. Nonetheless, the text did subtly support this mentality by the mere fact of requiring such a distinction and redefinition.

Sponsa Christi had called for an adjustment of the rules of cloister which had become too rigid. Formal guidelines for such adjustment were promulgated in a decree issued by the Congregation for Religious in 1956 entitled *Inter Cetera*. The purpose of the decree was to identify specific causes that would justify egress from or ingress into papal cloister. These included permission for superiors to oversee the physical plant of the monastery and to attend to essential business affairs outside the cloister, to visit a nun who was hospitalized, and to provide for the duties of externs who were lacking or impeded. Individuals were allowed to leave the monastery for medical treatment. This was a landmark decree in that it marked the first real change in the general law of cloister for nuns since the period immediately following the Council of Trent, and it was of immense pastoral consequence. All these provisions soon became common practice.

It is to be noted, however, that the theoretical distinction between communities wholly given to contemplation and others tended to overshadow, both canonically and psychologically, the very real fact that a departure from or entrance into cloister was to be a realistic and ordinary way of meeting essential needs of the community and of the individual, when these needs could not otherwise be reasonably provided for within the cloister. While the practical provisions of *Inter Cetera* appear as common sense to us, they continued to exist alongside a theoretical standard which distinguished these activities sharply from apostolic works, and thus they preserved the symbol of a state of life wholly given to contemplation while distinguishing it from that engaged in apostolic works. One might leave the enclosure to care for the needs of governance or of individuals, but any work involving persons outside the monastery when understood as ''apostolic'' was excluded by definition.

The juxtaposition of these two lines of development, one practical and one theoretical, both of which intended to strengthen and foster healthy canonical contemplative life, proved in short order to contain seeds of conflict—both practical and theoretical—which have not yet been resolved.

The distinction between contemplative communities wholly given to contemplation and those with a limited apostolate as well as the distinction between major and minor papal cloister interrupted the more organic life in some communities and precluded developments in others. The principle of integrity of charism, by which each order fostered contemplation through its own characteristic means and spirit so emphasized in *Sponsa Christi*, was overshadowed by this immediate requirement to define oneself in terms of cloister.

Implicit issues were not dealt with. For example, what about the apostolate of spiritual direction or the ministry of liturgical leadership or the extensive exercise of hospitality traditional in monasteries? *Sponsa Christi* was a serious call for renewal, and it provided for the needed adjustment in the cloister. Its weakness lay in the fact that communities had begun to define themselves in terms of major or minor cloister long before they began to renew themselves according to the principles outlined. This hindered many communities from recognizing and claiming their own traditional functions as apostolic and from developing such functions as their own proper means to and expression of the contemplative life. Thus, *Sponsa Christi* accidentally reinforced and preserved the symbol of the purely contemplative life, at the expense of a full flowering of the various charisms and the maturing of the different traditions from within, through their own experience, even as it opened the door to true renewal. Something similar occurred with Vatican II.

Beyond *Sponsa Christi*

Just eight years after *Inter Cetera*, the Second Vatican Council opened. The council took *Sponsa Christi* one step further. It had been the thrust of *Sponsa Christi* to initiate renewal of contemplative institutes as indicated above. Its practical instrument for this had been a clarification of the kinds of cloister and a strict definition of each. The council, however, explicitly moved beyond this constitution when, in *Perfectae Caritatis*, article 16, it called for the modification of cloister. This provision reflects the scope of the council's vision of the Church and its impact on all Church structures. Since the form of cloister had already undergone a radical updating as exemplified in *Inter Cetera*, and since this updating was just beginning during the years immediately before the council, it is clear that the council had in mind a genuine renewal and allowed for a growth that went far beyond *Sponsa Christi*.

The fact is, however that this has been contradicted since the close of the council. The course that has been followed is the very opposite of that envisioned by the council document. It began with the norms for implementation of *Perfectae Caritatis* in 1966, in which nuns were not given a structure for renewal similar to the Chapters of Renewal, which had the power to authorize experimentation for the apostolic religious communities. Rather, they were given a much more tentative mandate. Article 10 of *Ecclesiae Sanctae* states:

> If at times in monasteries of nuns certain experiments with respect to observances are judged opportune for an interval, these can be permitted by the superiors general or by delegates of the Holy See, and among Orientals by the patriarch or the lo-

cal hierarch. Yet special consideration should be given to the special outlook and frame of mind of those who are cloistered and who have so great a need for stability and security.

While it was the case that many monasteries still had not joined or formed federations and that several major orders had no superior general as such and, therefore, that the nuns would have had to work out their own way of collaborating, still there is a marked contrast between this approach to possible experimentation and the direct summons given to chapters of apostolic congregations. The language of valuation is used in article 10 to justify this "special" treatment. It is because the cloistered vocation is seen as requiring special protection and freedom from disturbance as well as being considered so important for the Church that it was and continues to be treated in a "special" way.

The Nature of the "Special Treatment." The nature of the special treatment given, however, reveals what is really at issue:

- The nuns have never been given permission to experiment.
- They have not been entrusted with the task of renewing their own structures from their own experience and in mutual collaboration.
- They have been warned about and discouraged from meeting and collaborating with religious of apostolic congregations and even with nuns of various traditions of contemplative life. (Grassroots efforts for interested monasteries to affiliate with the LCWR were aborted early on by a ruling of the Congregation for Religious.)
- The revision of their own constitutions has with few exceptions been directed from the outside: for some by a delegate of the male branch of the order—to which, however, they have no uniform relationship of obedience since monasteries are by tradition autonomous—and for others by the Congregation for Religious.

- The Congregation for Religious, prior to adequate consultation (since the review of constitutions was just getting underway), and therefore without allowing for any period of discernment or natural development and adaptation in the individual religious families, and prior to any authorization for experimentation, issued a decree on enclosure in 1969 entitled *Venite Seorsum*. This effectively eliminated any possibility of true experimentation or renewal of cloister practices—by defining before the fact what would and would not be possible and by introducing minute regulations on matters that were only beginning to be reviewed by the nuns.

- In cases where the delegates of the male branch of the order had made every effort to consult the nuns in assisting with the compilation of revisions for constitutions, the Congregation for Religious intervened over and over and ruled out key initiatives requested by the nuns in various parts of the world as these touched on enclosure. This is a critical point, since for practical purposes enclosure defines the whole lifestyle and affects every aspect of community life, relationships with family and other persons, education, health—physical and psychological—and the program of formation.

The principle of special privilege and special treatment has thus been used as a basis of discrimination—nuns being deprived of the autonomy given to other institutes—and control. Indeed, the measure of special privilege accorded in theory to contemplatives in the period before Vatican II became the measure of control exerted in their regard after the council. A case in point, but not an isolated one, may be the treatment recently given to the discalced Carmelite nuns. In October of 1984 the nuns were stunned to learn that Pope John Paul II had ordered CRIS to draw up legislation for them and that the basic framework of this text would be the Alcala Constitutions of 1581. A general consultation carried out between 1982 and 1983 by the Carmelite general superior, Felipe Sainz de Baranda, by order of the Pope, had revealed that eighty percent of the nuns desired that their new legislation be based on the Declarations, a legislative text written after Vatican II and approved by Pope Paul VI on an experimental basis for five years. Only twenty percent of the nuns, specifically seventy-three Carmels, two-thirds of them Spanish, wanted the 1581 Constitutions as the basic text. By his intervention the Pope removed from the Carmelite Order the task of preparing the new constitutional text, did not accept the project of legislation desired by the majority of the nuns, and implicitly judged the text approved by Pope Paul VI to be an inadequate expression of the Carmelite charism.

The radically distinct and discriminatory treatment given to nuns, a treatment which is diametrically opposed to the way contemplative institutes of men have governed and continue to govern themselves, reveals and illustrates the deep bias toward women that lies at the root of the problem. It illustrates clearly the fear of the transformation of symbols that is taking place inevitably within both Church and world.

A separate but equal tradition is, in fact, a separate and *un*equal tradition, as our own American history as well as political events in South Africa show. Such treatment, in the case of nuns, violates fundamental principles of justice. It is opposed, for example, to all that is written in *Pacem in Terris*, which opens with an affirmation of the equality of all persons, and to the entire tenor of the conciliar documents. Such discrimination is in essence a form of violence in the guise of protection and in the language of valuation. It presents itself as an effort to conserve the "treasure" of contemplative life—of nuns, be it noted, not necessarily of monks.

Despite all efforts during the rewriting of the Code of

Canon Law, during which the Association of Contemplative Sisters worked with all official channels, and despite the efforts of the Canon Law Society of America, the final edition of the new Code of Canon Law continues to separate and distinguish monks and nuns while it claims to see them as equal, a distinction that is totally uncalled for, is highly discriminatory in the present world, and can in no way provide the design for a Church of the future.

A Presumption of Bias. Because matters regarding enclosure and the vocation of nuns do not touch on any dogmatic or essential moral discipline or teaching of the Church, they illustrate all the more clearly the basic issues regarding the treatment of women in the Church and the profound need for reconciliation based on action.

Experience and historical reflection strongly indicate that nuns stand as a critical symbol in the mythology of the role of women in the Church. As such they have been made a symbolic pawn in the resistance to renewal. In the face of a clear summons to renewal, in the face of the highest authority of the Church—an ecumenical council in union with the Pope which called for change—Church authority centered in Rome has used its office to withdraw the institutes of nuns from the ordinary processes of renewal. It is as if the entire Church must renew but the nuns could only do so in a manner that was distinct and apart from the rest of the faithful, even apart from the process of other religious communities. The force of this resistance has been directed toward maintaining as far as possible the status quo for nuns. This is instructive, for it shows the depth of the myth ingrained in the psyche of the Western Church and the length to which every legitimate channel will be used—justly or unjustly—to maintain nuns in the place that is felt to be theirs.

This experience of limitation also indicates the nature of the myth of spirituality that was operative in the pre-Vatican II

Church, a myth which continues to challenge the ecclesiology of Vatican II. According to that myth, the other-worldly is the holy; the spirit is above the body; the materiality so innate in woman's nature can be made the symbol of the holy—but only through "material separation," which denies bodily reality and the incarnational character of the Christian experience and the unexpected action of the Holy Spirit. Closeness to God can only be achieved by distance from others. While this is not possible for those "in the world," the nuns still stand as the paradigm of holiness in their cloister.

All of this is very subtle, but it is evident consistently and clearly in the resistance that nuns have had to face from the time of the council in their efforts to renew their institution. The special intervention of the Pope in the case of the Carmelite Order—with respect to the nuns, let it be noted, and not to the friars—is only one instance of the interventions familiar to nuns since 1966. This resistance is out of proportion both to the number of persons in this style of life and to the nature of the issue of enclosure, and it is some indication of the deep psychic resistance to any change or transformation of the symbol of "the nun" and its special function as an ideal symbol of holiness. It indicates as well a deep resistance to the consequences of such a change, that is, to the changes now taking place in the status of women in the Christian community, changes which both precipitate and express a transformation of consciousness touching on the deepest perceptions of the Christian mystery. What is ultimately involved is a new understanding of the nature of holiness.

These patterns are unmistakable when viewed from the point of view of psychological dynamics, and it is helpful to take note of them in order to bring to light the real blocks to renewal in the Church and to the integration of the ecclesiology of Vatican II.

Summary of Part II

1. The history of the use of religious authority in the post-Vatican II Church to restrict renewal among the institutes of women dedicated to contemplative life is a history of discrimination. Authority has been used to maintain an oppressive control masked as protection. Its effect has been to support a type of spirituality foreign to that proposed by the council. This use of authority is well documented.

2. Any argument which attributes this discriminatory treatment over the past twenty years to the honest effort to serve the spiritual life of the nuns, and through them the whole Church, is belied by the actual facts of this twenty-year history. The latter is characterized by the efforts of the nuns to dialogue among themselves and to move as part of the Church with all the inherent struggles this involves. It is likewise characterized by their constant experience of exclusion in theory and in practice from the procedures, structures, and decision-making processes which affect their lives on a daily basis.

3. Because this history is so specific and contained, it is also useful as a paradigm in studying the real issue with which women are grappling in the Church and with which the Church itself struggles. That issue has to do with an ecclesiology, an *oeconomia*, which reflects the Church as a real household of the faith with both a fidelity to a hierarchical structure *and* a fidelity to the action of the Holy Spirit in persons as reflected in the multitude of charisms throughout the body of Christ. The former might be seen as characteristically male and the latter as characteristically female. Both are essential. But the fact that the latter is subject to so many restrictions, even to the extent of choking vital responses to the needs of people, is an indication that the Church is not open to women and to the values nurtured and embodied in women's gifts.

The experience of nuns accurately reflects the struggle between a former ecclesiology and a present one struggling for expression, between a former type of spirituality, individualistic and private and apart from the "world," and a present one which is open to the possibility of God's acting in our midst in new ways. It illustrates a painful and often hidden bias in the former ecclesiology which under the guise of an inadequate notion of the holy separated body from spirit, matter from mind, and most significantly, women, as more "im-mattered" or involved with the material reality of human life, from the symbols surrounding the holy.

This abstraction from the material reality of life under the guise of greater access to the holy or to the divine is epitomized in the symbol of the cloistered nun: the woman who stands as the most holy expression of the soul seeking God and who does so by being abstracted from, cut off from, "the world" through the instrumentality and the all-pervasive symbolism of the cloister, which makes her totally "other."

The real motivation of the heavy-handed effort to keep the cloistered nun totally cloistered in the traditional sense reveals itself in the means that have been employed in this effort.

4. The effort to keep nuns in what is perceived as "their place" without respect for their wishes, experience, or participation in the decision-making processes which affect their lives is an irreverence and an injustice. In addition, it has deprived the larger Christian community of a more spontaneous and closer association with the nuns in the post-Vatican II Church. It has hindered the fruitfulness and growth of women who are committed to the contemplative life and who try to operate from a communal stance of prayer and reflection on the gospel.

The need for centers of prayer, for close sharing of the Word of God with Catholics and those of other Christian Churches, the outreach to young people who seek contact with a living spiritual tradition—all of this has been hampered by the struggle the nuns have had to undergo in order to survive in a renewing Church while they themselves lack an official organ or adequate structure for renewal.

5. Questions are raised by this experience: Does the official, teaching Church really trust the sustained, communal attentiveness to the Word of God received, sifted, and purified in the communal and intercommunity context? Does it truly desire those who are committed to the Word by baptism and by profession of religious vows to respond in faith and courage to its demands? Does it wish to hear the reflected critique of contemplative women in the Church to the issues facing the Church in our society? Judging from the treatment received by the nuns, the answer would be no.

6. Because, in the case of the nuns, neither dogmatic nor moral issues are concerned, such as those surrounding marriage, abortion etc., the crucial issues are all the more clear. They involve rather the acceptance of women as equal members in the body of Christ; the relationship of the baptized to the ordinary authority of the Church, an authority intended by Christ to be one of service; and the integration of a new ecclesiology which reveals the Church as an organism and not as an authoritarian organization. The strength of opposition in the Church to this new ecclesiology has as its analogue the opposition in official quarters to the renewal of the institutes of nuns dedicated to the contemplative life.

Part III: Our Story—A Paradigm of Renewal

Our experience as contemplative women has brought us through eight distinct phases. The story of this process seems to constitute a paradigm for renewal that may be useful to others, and I summarize it as follows:

Phase 1: Call

The experience of the call to renewal in the context of the renewal of the Church came to us with *Sponsa Christi* in 1950 and with Vatican II.

Phase 2: Response

We responded to this call to renewal within communities, federations, and grassroots associations of contemplatives nationally and internationally.

Phase 3: Sin

The experience of sin in the Church attended this response. This involved the experience of being deprived of adequate renewal structures and excluded from these by law—a discriminatory pattern that marked postconciliar decrees and instructions. It involved, from 1969 onward, being harassed by letters from CRIS to our bishops and other delegates for nuns, letters which strove to deny the right of nuns of various orders to meet with one another in assemblies for the purposes of renewal. It involved the sabotage, on the part of CRIS, of even the minimal, consultative process of constitution revision carried on by the nuns, through legislation that blocked attempts to experiment or vetoed requested reforms in constitutions. This involved for us an experience of powerlessness and of oppression.

Phase 4: Process of Discernment and Struggle

There followed a struggle within our institutes to discern the proper course of action and the competence of rightful and competing authorities in the Church. These authorities included

a. the authority of the council itself and of the conciliar documents which were clear and comprehensive and of highest authority. These required taking positive steps toward renewal. They also required taking responsibility for the development of formation programs, for preservation and enhancement of the charism of the orders in keeping with historical and theological as well as sociological studies. From these responsibilities there could be no dispensation.

b. the authority of the local ordinaries operating under *Pastorale Munus*, paragraph 34, which for the first time since the Council of Trent gave local ordinaries personal jurisdiction (not merely delegated) over egress and ingress to the papal cloister of nuns. This accorded well with the first movements toward renewal in the local Church and led to fruitful dialogue with the bishops.

c. the authority of the Congregation for Religious which presented itself as the agent of the Pope, but whose procedures contradicted the mandates of the council.

Phase 5: Criteria for Discernment Clarified

Gradually it was realized that the competing demands were of two different orders, as were the competing authorities. It was realized that we had to accept the moral responsibility for our lives and for the health and well being of our communities and the candidates received in them in obedience to the clear direction of the council. It was also realized that, to do this adequately, we had to treat enclosure in an entirely different manner and this in the face of unbending pressure from CRIS. It must be recalled that the Poor Clares, for example, had a solemn vow of enclosure. This was a moment of moral conscience.

Phase 6: Risk Taking and Moral Decision

At the grassroots level, independently and in consultation with our bishops and other nuns, the various authorities within our communities—abbesses, prioresses, councils, and monastery chapters—began to assume, step by step, responsibility for their lives by acting to ensure that the spiritual, educational, and psychological needs of their sisters were evaluated and responded to. They did so even though this meant bypassing the directives that CRIS formulated and made great efforts to circulate—via the bishops, via the male branches of the orders, via extraordinary papal visitations, and via the constitutions that were drawn up without our active participation and without our approval. They did so even though they were deprived of any canonical permission to experiment such as had been not only permitted but requested of all other religious congregations in the Church.

This involved a great risk for us, one which touched our deepest sensibilities and perception of Church. It was, however, an act of inner freedom and moral conscience.

Phase 7: Critical Test of Our Choice

Only after having risked much by our decisions did we come to realize how oppressed we had been and how necessary such decisions were. In this critique of our own process the gospel principle proved most clarifying, namely, ''By their fruits you shall know them.''

Negative criteria. Prior to assuming responsibility for our own lives, we tried to ignore our needs or to meet them within the constrictions of the procedures of CRIS. This prompted a kind of codependency in the control mechanisms that were intended to prevent change and accentuated deep emotions in ourselves such as fear of change, inability to deal with others who did not want to change, isolation from one another, rash judgment of others' motives, a spirit of condemnation for any autonomous decision making on the part of others, and a deep anger born of a kind of passivity and resentment at the oppression that was operative but not recognized as such and dealt with. These negative fruits remain all too evident in communities that have not yet reached a place of inner freedom and independence in directing their own lives.

Positive criteria. The acknowledgement of our responsibilities and the effort to meet them out of our own consciences resulted in greater peace in communities, greater tolerance and ability to relate to others and to other communities who chose to proceed in a different manner, a capacity for unity in diversity, a sense of vitality and interest in our vocation, energetic cultivation of the resources among the nuns, a sense of hope in the new members of the orders. This situation perdures even though we have no bodies of law which represent our actual practice and which we can present honestly to our sisters in formation.

Phase 8: Sense of Solidarity

This entire process has given us a sense of solidarity with other women in the Church as well as with all who face the challenge of growth and renewal. After having lived through this process painfully and alone, we find that we can support and encourage this process in others who meet the same dilemma of a double standard and of the conflicts which arise from the presence of competing ecclesiologies in the Church.

Part IV: Summary Conclusions

In preaching, in attitudes, and in spiritual direction the vocation of the nuns has been treated as something set apart and, prior to the council, as set above the vocation to Christian marriage and even above the call to other kinds of vowed life.

This appeared as the highest form of valuation.

That some other dynamic was in fact present is made evident in the resistance that has been made by official structures outside the orders to any change in the institution of nuns, even though such was mandated by Vatican Council II.

Since such resistance has been shown only to the institutes of contemplative nuns in this particular way, it is clear that they are viewed as untouchable symbols of the holiness or ideal of Christian life. The efforts to control their further development through use of authority is an effort to resist the spirituality of Vatican II. Somehow, even if unconsciously, it is perceived that if this symbol is altered the myth that surrounds the vocation of women, the place of women in the Church, will be destroyed, and the Church will be vulnerable to the demands of the new ecclesiology which requires that women be treated as equals in the Church as is their prerogative. That such is the case and that the consequences of real change in contemplative orders would entail a radical transformation in the Church is sensed, and it is this that provides the energy behind the exclusion of nuns from the project of renewal in any official way.

I would venture to say that all these struggles witness to the journey that the Christian community is making across uncharted frontiers. We are already across the threshold of a new time, one which calls us to a fuller participation in and understanding of the profound mystery of Christ. As we move forward, I expect a rediscovery of what our life in Christ involves and the experience within our world and time of the power, the surprise, the unbelievable grace that is God's gift to us in Christ.

Notes

1. Pastoral on Women hearings. Statement of the National Board of the Leadership Conference of Women Religious. Presented to the ad hoc Committee of Bishops, Washington, March 4–5, 1985. *Origins* 14, no. 40 (March 21, 1985) 653–56.

2. This double principle of adaptation of cloister along with maintenance of the withdrawal from the world in the practice of the contemplative life is affirmed in more general terms in *Perfectae Caritatis*, art. 7.

3. This interesting history is traced in "The Cloister" by Valentine Theodore Schaaf, *Canon Law Studies* no. 13 (Cincinnati: St. Anthony Messenger Press, 1921).

4. See "Violation of the Cloister" by Garrett Francis Barry, *Canon Law Studies* no. 148 (Washington: The Catholic University of America Press, 1942).

5. *Perfectae Caritatis*, art. 9 reads in sentence 1 and ff.: "In the East and in the West, the *venerable institution of monastic life* should be faithfully preserved, and should grow ever-increasingly radiant with its own authentic spirit. Through the *long course of the centuries* this institution has proved its merits splendidly to the Church and to human society. The main task of *monks* is to render to the Divine Majesty a service at once simple and noble, within the monastic confines . . ." (italics mine).

6. The present text and the theology it expresses are the result of intense debate during the early months of the council between two points of view on how the role of Mary should be articulated to express best the honor that is her due. One tendency was to emphasize Mary's uniqueness in relation to the Church by issuing a separate document on the role of the Mother of God. The other was to show Mary's inseparable connection with the Church and all the redeemed, and to do so by inserting the description of her role within the constitution on the Church. In keeping with the ecclesiology developed by the council, the latter tendency prevailed. The fact that it caused such heated debate witnesses to the transition occurring in the theology of the Church. See *Lumen Gentium*, art. 53, and n. 256 in *The Documents of Vatican II*, ed. Walter M. Abbott, trans. Joseph Gallagher (New York: The America Press, 1966) 85.

7. Article 18 of *Ad Gentes* reads: "Right from the planting stage of the Church, the religious life should be carefully fostered . . . . Working to plant the Church, and thoroughly enriched with the *treasures of mysticism adorning the Church's religious tradition*, religious communities should strive to give expression to these treasures. . . . Let them reflect attentively on how Christian religious life may be able to assimilate *the ascetic and contemplative tradition whose seeds were sometimes already planted by God in ancient cultures prior* to the preaching of the gospel.

"Worthy of special mention are the various projects aimed at helping *the contemplative life take root*. There are those who while retaining the essential elements of monastic life are bent on implanting the very rich traditions of their own order. Others are returning to simpler forms of ancient monasticism. But all are striving to work out a *genuine adaptation to local conditions*. For the contemplative life belongs to the fullness of the Church's presence . . ." (italics mine).

*V*ilma Seelaus, O.C.D., of the Carmel of Barrington, Rhode Island, reflects on the renewal of attitudes and structures taking place and yet to take place in contemplative communities as a consequence of a fuller understanding of their role in the Church and in the world. Sister Vilma makes it clear that contemplation that leads to global vision, to nonviolence, to peace, to conversion, to forgiveness, is not limited to those in contemplative communities. It is for all. She notes that through an "appropriate visibility" such communities better serve as reflectors and reminders to the Church of its contemplative dimension and call. Sister Vilma looks not only to the future of religious life but to the future of the Church and of planet earth which, she implies, depends upon each person's rediscovery of his or her "contemplative roots."

8

Toward a More Contemplative Church

Vilma Seelaus, O.C.D.

The least understood of all areas of religious commitment and service in the Church is contemplative life. Yet, that its significance be grasped is imperative to the life of the Church, for as the great theologian Karl Rahner has written, "the Christian of the future will be a contemplative or he [sic] will cease to be anything at all."[1] While these words challenge all of us, they have special meaning for the future of contemplative religious life.

Past expressions of religious life focused on the concept of separation from the world. For contemplatives, enclosure with its high walls, grills, and dark curtains dramatically imaged such separation. For the most part, contemplatives were either considered among the elite—because prayer put them above the rest of the Church—or they were dismissed as irrelevant.

Vatican II, in declaring the universal call to holiness and by inviting all Christians to discover their contemplative roots,[2] laid the foundations for a contemporary theology of contemplative life. New concepts of cloister necessarily followed. No longer could contemplatives, by their life of prayer, salve the

133

conscience of others for their dearth of prayer. Rather, they began to declare themselves reflectors within the Church and society of the contemplative dimension inherent in the human.

Jesus the contemplative invites all of us into the intimacy of his relationship with Abba, his father. From this relationship flowed Jesus' sense of identity, mission, and capacity for compassionate love even unto death. Contemplative life carries on in time and through history the prayer of Jesus within a lifestyle that privileges contemplative prayer.

But today contemplatives are also challenged by a growing desire to reflect to others their own contemplative dimension.[3] As a result of this fuller understanding of their place in today's world, they see the need for an appropriate visibility within the Church community which would clearly demonstrate solidarity in prayer as the grounding of Christian discipleship. If contemplative life needs to show a different face from the one it showed in centuries past, it is because of the conviction contemplatives have today that the future of the Church depends on the Church's rediscovery of its contemplative roots. Contemplation is not an esoteric pastime but the very warp and woof of the Church's life.

Contemplation that cannot be realized in the midst of everyday life is meaningless for the vast majority of humankind. Therefore, a lifestyle among contemplatives that suggests the esoteric, or elitism, is incongruous with its deeper message: that contemplation is at the heart not only of the Church but of all that is human. Our challenge for today as contemplatives is to retrieve for humankind its contemplative consciousness. This means we must embody prayer in a lifestyle that symbolically awakens in others their intrinsic desire for God. Consequently, fidelity for contemplatives lies not in preserving past structures but in fostering the life's deepest meaning: union with the divine within themselves for the Church.

The paradox of contemplation manifests itself in the intensity with which oneness with others is experienced. Boundaries dissolve and compassion expands. The "God and I alone" language of the mystics does not reflect the fullness of their contemplative experience, as a comprehensive reading of their works discloses. The mystics, even within the limited cosmology of their era, were the forerunners of global vision.[4] Privatized prayer may be a phase in a person's development, but it is not the full realization of one's contemplative dimension. Inevitably, contemplation unites a person not only with God but with all that is authentically human. In Christ, God—the divine incomprehensible mystery—is definitively present to the human endeavor.[5] The presence of Christ in our prayer both challenges and becomes a corrective to the deformations brought on by our own and others' finite and thus limited and imperfect—sometimes violent—responses to life. The infinite capacity for God that is ours in Christ wears away the limits of human finitude and stretches the human ability for peacemaking and compassionate solidarity.[6] Contemplative communities, through the sincerity of their efforts to foster community and generate peacefulness within and among themselves, offer the hope that such peaceful living together is possible for the human community.

Religious life in the United States actually began as a contemplative venture. The first religious invited to make a foundation in the original thirteen colonies were the Carmelites, who settled near Baltimore in 1790. Symbolically, by being the first to arrive, these women gave expression to the contemplative grounding of all religious life. Many founders of apostolic communities were inspired by the mystics of contemplative orders. The need to revise monastic customs incompatible with active ministry does not negate the equally important need for apostolic congregations to get in touch again with the congregations' contemplative roots.

Thérèse of Lisieux discovered the meaning of her life in the image of the heart. The heart is the life-force of the body/person, the center from which love emanates. Therefore, in ecstatic serendipity, Thérèse exclaims, "In the heart of the Church, my Mother, I shall be love."[7] To mirror Love is the Christian call.

While those in active ministry may need to point the Church's vision prophetically toward future possibilities, contemplatives sustain the heart of things. Contemplation hardly exists without vision, and contemplatives also press forward toward the "not yet." But their primary focus is to move ever more deeply into the divine center where past, present, and future converge in a harmonious whole. Their challenge, as the Church community moves into the future, is to treasure as part of the vision what others by stressing a more single focus may in time need to retrieve.

Practically, what might these reflections mean for the future of contemplative life in the United States? They mean, first of all, that authentic renewal has yet to begin. A false separation ethos still enshrouds many contemplatives, in spite of invitations from the Church to reflect more clearly its contemplative center. At the same time, change of itself does not ensure a deeper contemplative insertion into the Church's life.

As post-Vatican II contemplatives, the inner dynamic of our traditional way of life both invites and challenges us. A place where *silence* and *solitude* can truly be experienced is essential.[8] Noise pollution and the superficial togetherness characteristic of today's culture close off deeper levels of the human potential for God. Contemplatives can value the communications media and sound technology without succumbing to their fascination. These must not be used to avoid solitude or the pain of God's often searing, purifying presence. Personal purification is never solipsistic. It issues forth like a centrifugal force to engage mysteriously the human community with whom we are one. In contemplative presence to God the boundaries of the one and the many dissolve. Therefore, the movement toward a creative harmony among silence, solitude, and contemplative presence to one another and the Church community is especially challenging for us today as contemplatives.

If the desire for solitude is not a luxury but the inner imperative of a heart longing for union with God, from similar depth comes desire for authentic community. Both are integral to shaping the future. The secular world is slowly recognizing the value of and the need for community, and foundations for community building gain momentum.[9]

Genuine community fosters human/spiritual growth and, conversely, as individuals grow community life is strengthened. Community structures and the exercise of authority exist to faithfully serve, not to arbitrarily constrain human freedom. The dynamism of contemplative community life is centered within the purpose that brings the members together. Rules and constitutions are servants of this ultimate goal: a life of prayer rooted in gospel values for the Church/world. Should either individuals or the group lose sight of their purpose, becoming either legalistic or laissez faire, community life disintegrates into backbiting or superficial camaraderie.

Just as solitude is not a luxury, neither are efforts toward community building. Intrinsic to being a follower of Jesus is willingness to sit at table with tax collectors and sinners.[10] The physiognomy of most communities is diverse indeed and is a microcosm of the global community. To add a personal note, here in the Barrington Carmel we represent equally north and south, with members from west to east coast. Ethnically we are diverse; consequently, "sitting together at table" is not always easy. Potential for a mini–civil war, even for a nuclear holocaust, is as much a reality for us as it is whenever people come together, as the history of secular and religious life demonstrates. But our God is more powerful and gracious than we are weak. The indwelling spirit of Jesus encourages, strengthens, challenges, and enables us to be women of peace, to receive into our hearts the eschatological blessing of the Christ who presides at this community gathering, so that divine compassionate love can be increasingly the root and foundation of our lives together.

Today contemplatives are called to model communities of nonviolence, allowing Christ to turn the swords of anger, resentment, and bitterness into plowshares. Psychological and spiritual helps toward inner peace must be provided. World peace begins in the heart of individuals.

Entering a contemplative lifestyle intensifies the human need for conversion and for acceptance and integration of one's shadow. The intensity of living together with the same persons year after year, day after day, uncovers our woundedness and mirrors our defenses. One has little psychological room to hide in if one is open, honest, and willing to be vulnerable. Christ in our midst continually calls us to acceptance of our incompleteness, to forgiveness of ourselves and others, and to surrender to divine compassionate love. Through this process are we enabled to accept others in their incompleteness. Communities rooted in peacemaking provide a nucleus for world peace and a model for harmonious living in a violent, war-torn world.

Concepts of cloister and the fact that contemplative monasteries are autonomous and generally lack a central government within the order have helped to foster isolationism and authoritarian leadership within contemplative monasteries. Where one might expect feminine consciousness, discipleship of equals, and relationships of mutuality to flourish, instead, Church patriarchal structures are paralleled with a matriarchal system that inevitably limits human growth. A serious question facing those who value their contemplative call, yet who are conscious of the limitations of past structures, deals with the human developmental growth process. Traditional structures allow little room for temporary growth needs which, if realized, could open the person to a fuller contemplative experience. Discovering ways of sustaining traditional values and at the same time creatively responding to the human developmental process presents a serious contemporary challenge.

Contemplative communities with awakened feminine consciousness often find little support in their diocesan setting. Some communities have played a leadership role in revising sexist language and the exclusively masculine symbols for God found in liturgical worship and the Liturgy of the Hours. Contemplatives whose prayer has disclosed for them both the masculine and the feminine within the God of incomprehensible mystery find it difficult to pray with exclusively masculine symbols for God. Vision of a future where women and men cooperate in a relationship of equality and mutuality challenge present structures which, for the most part, confine decision making and official discourse regarding the order's charism to its male branch. Communities with awakened feminine consciousness become places of worship and sources of encouragement for laywomen who struggle with a Church at times insensitive to them.

Well-educated women, many of whom leave a successful career, enter contemplative life today. Some enter with graduate degrees in theology or Scripture. The writings of the mystics describe the contemplative experience as mystical theology. In the future, greater interaction between contemplatives and theologians could enrich theology. Dialogue between the religious experience of contemplatives and the speculations of theologians could either validate the understanding and vision of each or help bring each other to a deeper truth.[11]

To foster spiritual awakening, work toward reappropriating the mystical writings of each tradition is imperative for contemplatives. Their meaning for today can be lost because the language and symbol are of another time and culture. A new hermeneutic is called for if these classics are to be more accessible to those experiencing spiritual hunger today. Study of interpretation theories is therefore important for at least some contemplatives if such work is to be furthered.[12]

Mysticism is at the heart of all world religions. It effects a deep, spontaneous bonding between persons of different cultures and beliefs. Interreligious dialogue between Christian and Buddhist and Hindu monastics is a present reality with an expansive future. The philosophy and meditation praxis of Eastern religions as well as the exemplary dedication of their renunciates both affirm and critique our own Christian monastic tradition. The North American Board for East-West Dialogue charts a future for intensive exchange and mutual enrichment.[13]

Contemplatives are the praying heart of the Church who continue through time the prayer of Jesus. The vision of Jesus "that all be one" must therefore truly be theirs. What this means for today and the future has implications beyond past envisioning. A mode of consciousness which links one to the entire cosmos through intuitive awareness of the oneness of all life—the interdependence of its multiple manifestations, its cycles of change and transformation—offers not only a language and symbol for spirituality of the future but also practical imperatives for a reverent, ecologically minded way of living.[14]

That all are one is the contemplative experience. Transpersonal consciousness and experiential awareness of human solidarity breaks down barriers of the "we and they." "What you do to others you do to me" is the Jesus experience become ours. The anguish of powerlessness before massive global injustice brings a cry to the heart like the total abandon of Jesus to his Abba. In that cry, for us as for Jesus, is the thunder of resurrection.

Far from being irrelevant, contemplative life, like a global womb, must help carry humankind into a future transformed by justice, peace, and compassionate love. Indeed, all persons of the future must be contemplatives or planet earth may be no more.

Notes

1. Karl Rahner, *Theological Investigations* (New York: Seabury Press, 1971) 7:31. Karl Rahner made a major contribution toward our understanding of the presence of God to human life. See "Experience of Self and Experience of God," *Theological Investigations* (London: Darton, Longman and Todd, 1961–76) 13:124–25.

2. See *The Documents of Vatican II*, ed. Walter M. Abbott, (New York: Guild Press, 1966). Numerous texts indicate the universal call to holiness and its implications. To cite a few:

Constitution	Article	Paragraph	Page in Abbott
Lumen Gentium	10	1	27
	11	6	29
	35	2	61
	36	3	62
	40	-	66–67
	42	-	70–71
	48	5	79–80
	50	3	82
	65	1	93
On Divine Revelation	8	2	116
	14–16	-	121–22
On the Sacred Liturgy	1–4	-	137–38
	10–12	-	142–43
Gaudium et Spes	4	-	201–02
	8	2	206
	14	3	212

3. In a historic meeting of contemplatives from the United States and Canada in August 1969 at Woodstock, Maryland, where for the first time contemplatives of different orders met together, the desire

to reflect by their lives the importance of the contemplative dimension emerged as a common urgency. This meeting gave birth to the Association of Contemplative Sisters.

4. At an international symposium, *The Monk as Universal Archetype*, held at Holyoke, Mass. November 1980, a scientist observed: "Mystics are the world's greatest plagiarizers. They said four hundred years ago what scientists will be saying tomorrow." See Raimundo Panikkar, *Blessed Simplicity: The Monk as Universal Archetype* (New York: Seabury Press, 1982).

5. See Franz Josef van Beeck, "The Human Concerns: Included and Made Obedient," *Christ Proclaimed: Christology as Rhetoric* (New York: Paulist Press, 1979) 144-83.

6. See Vilma Seelaus, *Prayer and Human Liberation, Teresa's Way of Peacemaking in a Nuclear Age* and *Teresa's Inner Journey to Transformed Consciousness* (Canfield, Ohio: Alba House Communications, 1986, 1987, 1988). These audio-tapes show how Teresa was both formed and deformed by the culture in which she lived. Teresa's prayer relationship with Christ proved a corrective for the deformation of the culture. Through a life transformed in Christ, and through her work in founding monasteries, Teresa contributed to the culture's transformation.

7. *The Autobiography of St. Thérèse of Lisieux: Story of a Soul,* trans. John Clarke, (Washington: ICS Publications, Institute of Carmelite Studies, 1975-76) 194.

8. Praying in solitude a portion of the Liturgy of the Hours, specifically Midmorning, Midafternoon and Night Prayer, provides a rhythm of solitude and community. Weekly hermit days and community and individual hermit retreats also contribute toward this rhythm.

9. See M. Scott Peck, M.D., *The Different Drum: Community Making and Peace* (New York: Simon and Schuster, 1987). Peck is the founder of the Foundation for Community Encouragement, a nonprofit organization for promoting community and world understanding.

10. In Judaism, fellowship at table had the special meaning of fellowship in the sight of God. Each person at the table ate a piece of broken bread and thus received a share in the blessing spoken by the master of the house over the whole loaf. Finally, every meal is a sign of the coming eschatological meal and the eschatological fellowship with God. The inclusion of sinners in the community of salvation,

achieved in table fellowship, is the most meaningful expression of the redeeming love of God. See Walter Kasper, *Jesus the Christ* (New York: Paulist Press, 1977) 101–02.

11. Teresa of Avila is the classic example of a contemplative whose religious experience influenced theologians of her day regarding spiritual theology. Examples of this are found in all of her writings. See *The Collected Works of St. Teresa of Avila*, trans. Otilio Rodriguez and Kieran Kavanaugh (Washington: ICS Publications, Institute of Carmelite Studies, 1980) 2:24–25.

12. Such is the task of The Carmelite Forum, a small group of theologians, historians of the order, psychologists, and translator of the texts, a group that includes nuns and friars, calced and discalced. As a result of their work together, the beginnings of an audio-tape library on the collected works of the Carmelite mystics, and other printed works as well, are now available from Alba House Publications, Canfield, Ohio.

13. The North American Board for East-West Dialogue is a subcommission of the International Secretariate A.I.M. (Aide Inter Monasteres) of the Benedictine Confederation.

14. *The Global Brain* (Hartley Film Foundation, Cos Cob, CT), a multimedia presentation based on Peter Russell's book of that title, presents the idea of the earth as an integrated, self-regulating, living organism and considers what function the human race may be playing in the planetary system.